PENGUIN BOOKS

PAPPYLAND

Wright Thompson is a senior writer for ESPN and the bestselling author of *Pappyland* and *The Cost of These Dreams*. He lives in Oxford, Mississippi, with his family.

* * *

Praise for *Pappyland*

One of ABC News's Best Books of the Year
One of *Garden & Gun*'s Favorite Books for Southerners in 2020

"A soulful journey that blends together biography, autobiography, philosophy, Kentucky history, the story of bourbon's origins, and an insider's look at how the Van Winkle whiskey is made and marketed . . . Thompson, an ESPN senior writer by way of Mississippi, comes off as the Boswell of bourbon country here—a keen literary observer and respectful fanboy with an obvious affection for his subject. . . . *Pappyland* moves smoothly through the family lore with the subtle nuances of a well-aged bourbon; it has top notes of stoicism and melancholy and a lingering finish of pride, even when recounting the hard times."
—*The New York Times Book Review*

"A warm and loving reflection that, like good bourbon, will stand the test of time."
—Eric Asimov, *The New York Times*

"Over the years spent reporting on the Van Winkles, Thompson pondered not only their impeccable talents, but also their sense of fun, as when they sneak the good stuff into the Kentucky Oaks by pouring it into a Seven Seas salad dressing bottle. Thompson's time with them raised questions about his own family, revealing how ambition can draw both light and darkness, and how some of the greatest stories ever told are just perfectly aged, delicious myths."
—*Garden & Gun*

"*Pappyland* is as invigorating as the smell of freshly cut Kentucky blue-grass, and goes down as smoothly as a glass of Pappy's beloved bourbon."
—*Shelf Awareness*

"One of Wright Thompson's many gifts is his ability to give language to those intangibles of life that are, to the rest of us, indescribable. So his account of the Van Winkle family and their elusive, masterful bourbon is justly rendered in profound, utterly compelling fashion. Success and failure; legacy and sacrifice; the commitments to family and the fight to reclaim something lost to time—*Pappyland* fits neatly alongside the traditions and scope of great Southern literature and, like the bourbon at the center of the story, captures a special kind of lightning in a bottle."
—Ashley Christensen, James Beard Award–winning chef, fan of brown water on ice with a lemon twist

"A fast-paced and colorful history of twentieth-century Southern culture, told through the story of charismatic cult-bourbon maker Julian P. Van Winkle III . . . 'Being Southern,' Thompson writes, 'means carrying a responsibility to shake off the comforting blanket of myth and see ourselves clearly.' Thompson more than fulfills that burden with insight and eloquence."
—*Publishers Weekly* (starred review)

"A lyrical journey through the life of bourbon's down-to-earth royalty."
—Jonathan Karl, *The Wall Street Journal*'s Leaders' Favorite Books of 2020

"A bourbon-laced Book of Hours heady with history, soul-searching, Southern shrines, and meditations on fatherhood. Thompson goes in search of Kentucky's most potent heritage and slowly circles round to his own. It's a story meant for sipping, rough and sweet on the tongue."
—Burkhard Bilger

"Frankly I don't give a damn about bourbon. But I do care greatly about family and children, about fathers and sons, and about tradition and legacy, and it's out of these ingredients that Wright Thompson distills this beautiful and life-loving book. *Pappyland* is the story of bourbon master Julian Van Winkle, told by a master writer reaching across generations for meaning. Which means it is nothing less than the story of mastery itself."

—Tom Junod

"Only Wright Thompson could tell the story of something as beloved as Pappy and make me admire it more. This is a profound book that is every bit as nuanced and lasting as the whiskey it's about. It made me reconsider the power of mythology, history, family legacy, and the stories we tell ourselves. I also learned a lot about fine bourbon."

—Eli Saslow, winner of the Pulitzer Prize and author of *Rising Out of Hatred*

"In *Pappyland* Wright Thompson takes his reader on a journey, indeed a pilgrimage, across times, places, and generations all deeply rooted in the bluegrass country of Kentucky in search of the almost mythical Pappy Van Winkle. In elegant prose Thompson embarks on an odyssey which, like all such endeavors, ultimately returns the hero to home, both for his subject, Julian Van Winkle III, and for the author."

—Dr. Paul M. Pearson, director of the Thomas Merton Center

"An amiable journey, courtesy of ESPN sportswriter Thompson, into the arcana of American whiskey . . . If you're a fan of the magic that is an artful bourbon, this is just the book for you." —*Kirkus Reviews*

"In Wright Thompson's beautifully written and delightful book, Julian Van Winkle's odyssey to make whiskey in the spirit of his beloved Pappy becomes a story about how we keep faith with the past—with our ancestors and with the legacy of a great craft—and how we move on from it. *Pappyland* is a beautiful antidote to false sentiment; I cherished it."

—Walter Isaacson

ALSO BY WRIGHT THOMPSON

The Cost of These Dreams

PENGUIN BOOKS
An imprint of Penguin Random House LLC
penguinrandomhouse.com

First published in the United States of America by Penguin Press,
an imprint of Penguin Random House LLC, 2020
Published in Penguin Books 2022

ISBN 9780735221277 (paperback)

THE LIBRARY OF CONGRESS HAS CATALOGED THE HARDCOVER EDITION AS FOLLOWS:
Names: Thompson, Wright, author.
Title: Pappyland: A Story of Family, Fine Bourbon,
and the Things That Last / Wright Thompson.
Description: New York: Penguin Press, 2020.
Identifiers: LCCN 2020004081 (print) | LCCN 2020004082 (ebook) |
ISBN 9780735221253 (hardcover) | ISBN 9780735221260 (ebook)
Subjects: LCSH: Van Winkle, Julian, III. | Old Rip Van Winkle Distillery—
History. | Whiskey industry—Kentucky.
Classification: LCC HD9395.U474 O4384 2020 (print) |
LCC HD9395.U474 (ebook) | DDC 338.7/66352 [B]—dc23
LC record available at https://lccn.loc.gov/2020004081
LC ebook record available at https://lccn.loc.gov/2020004082

Printed in the United States of America
1 3 5 7 9 10 8 6 4 2

BOOK DESIGN BY DANIEL LAGIN
MAP BY MEIGHAN CAVANAUGH

PAPPYLAND

A Story of Family,
Fine Bourbon,
and the
Things That Last

Wright Thompson

PENGUIN BOOKS

For Pappy and Dad

—JVW

For Wallace and Louise

—WWT

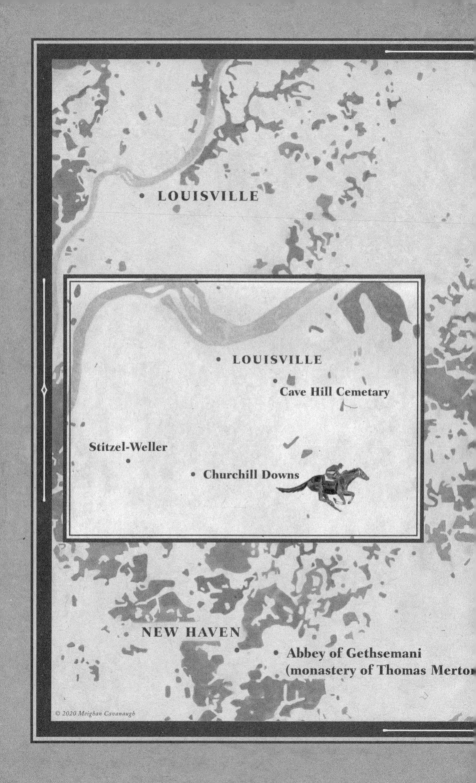

LOUISVILLE

LOUISVILLE

Cave Hill Cemetary

Stitzel-Weller

Churchill Downs

NEW HAVEN

Abbey of Gethsemani
(monastery of Thomas Merton)

© 2020 Meighan Cavanaugh

Buffalo Trace Distillery

FRANKFORT •

LEXINGTON
•

Lawrenceburg Bottling Plant

PAPPYLAND

Then inside the cave he could hear the gypsy starting to sing and the soft chording of a guitar. *"I had an inheritance from my father,"* the artificially hardened voice rose harshly and hung there.

Then went on:

> *"It was the moon and the sun*
> *And though I roam all over the world*
> *The spending of it's never done."*

—ERNEST HEMINGWAY,
For Whom the Bell Tolls

PART I

- 1 -

ON THE AFTERNOON of the Kentucky Oaks, I searched the grandstand at Churchill Downs for Julian P. Van Winkle III. It was Friday, the day before the Derby, and it looked like it might just stay beautiful and clear, a miracle this time of year in the humid South. As I made my way through a crowd of people with a sheen on their faces and seersucker stuck to their thighs, I thought of an old friend who once said that existing at our latitude felt like living inside someone's mouth. The breath of racehorses, summer humidity, Kentucky Straight Bourbon Whiskey—the South has many forms of heat, by-products of a place perched delicately on the edge between romance and hypocrisy. The Ole Miss band used to play a slow version of "Dixie" before the game, and even as I winced at the Confederate nostalgia, I also teared up because the song reminded me of my father. That's what Patterson Hood called the "Duality of the Southern Thing." The Derby distills those feelings.

When horses turn for home, we are all wild and free, sweating and cheering, the dream on our breath and clutched in our fists. I admit I love that blood-sport rush.

The pageant of the big race swirled around me. The old Louisville families gathered in boxes along the stretch, gripping drinks and pari-mutuel tickets. I was at the track to write racing columns for my magazine and Julian was living another day in what seemed to be the endless spring break of his life. I didn't know him yet. We had met several times before to discuss a book about bourbon we wanted to write together. I was to help him tell the story of his bourbon, the mythical and rare Pappy Van Winkle, but it became clear that there was no way to separate the bourbon's mythology from his personal history. That clarity lay before me. At the moment, I just needed to find the man in the madness at Churchill Downs.

I finally found him holding court in a box about halfway up the grandstand surrounded by old friends, a well-tailored blue-and-white-striped sport coat draped across his shoulders and reading glasses dangling from his neck beneath a peach-colored, whiskey barrel–patterned bow tie. Julian kept on-brand with his Pappy ball cap, and a lifetime of May afternoons in Kentucky had taught him to put on duck boots before heading to the track. He smiled when he saw me and handed me his flask of Weller 12. The whiskey went down smooth, with enough burn to let you know it was working, which was what my father used to say when he'd disinfect my cuts with hydrogen peroxide. Julian loves the 12-year-old

Weller. He's got a storage facility full of it—and a bourbon club's fantasy of other rare bourbons. If you ask him where he keeps it, he'll wink and laugh and dissemble, but he won't give out the coordinates. "I went to the shed," he said. "My whiskey shed, the storage shed, whose location will remain anonymous. I'll show you a picture of it."

His wife, Sissy, saw me and waved. I think I might be in love with her. She's pretty, with a great laugh. Her smile is an invitation to pull up a seat. I had stepped into a party that had been raging for a generation or two. They had a bag of chocolates and a Seven Seas salad dressing bottle filled with bourbon. Julian often travels with his own booze. Wouldn't you? He is famous among friends for showing up at parties with half-pints of Pappy—used for tasting and testing barrels—and passing them around. They're called blue caps. I love the blue caps. Once, before I was about to give a speech, his son, Preston, handed me one to take onstage. I have this memory of Julian at a food and wine festival after-party—it was at a local Indian restaurant that had been turned into a Bollywood dance club—and he was floating around the dance floor, hands in the air, pausing only to give anyone who wanted a pull of the Pappy he kept in his pocket. In that moment, I wanted to know how someone got to be so free and if that freedom created his perfect whiskey, or the other way around. That night exists as a kind of psychedelic dream to me, the feeling of being whisked away in a black Suburban and ending up with streaky images of dancing and music and Pappy.

Julian looks more and more like Pappy every day. He's got a silver cuff of hair around his bald head and is quick with a joke, usually on himself. On his right hand, he wears a family ring just like the one his grandfather and father wore. The Van Winkles have a large number of traditions, the most famous of which is their whiskey. That fame doesn't make it any more or less important than the others. They are all just the things this old Southern family does in the course of being itself.

Among Julian's many quirks: wearing fake rotten teeth, which he and Sissy sported each time they first met a set of future in-laws of one of their three daughters; searching for records to fit his old-timey jukebox in the basement; listening to music while cleaning out the big silver pots after frying Thanksgiving turkeys; setting mole traps for going on forty years now, without ever successfully catching a mole; and firing a paintball gun at the deer on his property that want to tear up his plants. One night, deep into two open bottles of bourbon, he grabbed a flashlight and I grabbed the paintball assault rifle and we went out into the neighborhood. I kept the weapon up like they do in the war movies and he swung the light through the trees. We didn't see anything. I was bummed. He was stoic, as usual.

Julian almost never complains—few people know, for instance, that he's just on the other side of cancer treatment that could have ended very differently. Normally a private man, he allowed his closest friends to see the fear in his eyes; to share in his vulnerability. His illness made him newly reflective, which would have a cascade of repercussions in his life. He'd reached the point when he had to take dying seriously. Everyone passes through that valley and everyone emerges changed. His bourbon is passing through a valley, too. In the coming months, he will taste the new liquor that will fill his bottles. The whiskey that built his success had run out, and the "new whiskey," distilled and laid up many years ago, is now finally ready to be tasted and, with luck, bottled. I would come to appreciate the challenge of dealing with market trends when your product gets made as many as twenty-five years in the past. When I met Julian this is what loomed largest; soon it would be time for him to test the first ever Pappy Van Winkle's Family Reserve made from whiskey distilled by his partner Buffalo Trace. Whiskey is marketed as an antidote to change, so the magic is especially vulnerable during times of transition. That tension ran through my mind during this otherwise carefree day at the nation's most famous racetrack. Julian was looking far into the future, to see how this brand and whiskey would be passed from one generation to the next. The Van Winkles have done most things very well, except for that: the last time the baton pass got seriously fucked up.

But on this afternoon Julian was in good humor: passing around whiskey, cracking jokes, waiting on the bugle to blow, being Julian Van Winkle. From our box seats, the crowd around us kept an eye on the infield scoreboard, counting down the minutes until post for the next race. People killed time with liquor and stories. A local doctor juggled apples, taking the occasional bite without missing a rotation as we cheered him on.

Finally the next race began with a thunder of hooves. There's a word that describes that sound, *rataplan*, which evokes the incredible noise a dozen running horses can make and the way you feel that noise in your chest, loud—not like something in nature but like standing next to a tower of speakers at an Allman Brothers show. The sound takes on physical form and lives on as psychic echo. The crowd roared and leaned in. We stopped to look down at the track as the horses left the gate and came bounding past. It took less than two minutes, the crowd swaying, clutching the white betting slips, matching numbers to silks, standing and screaming beneath the roof of the grandstand. Oh, glorious afternoon!

Churchill Downs has been expanded over the years, the luxury suites rising high above the spires—an unintentional and dark metaphor about the change that has come to this track. This new-money Derby attracts people who seem desperate for the lifestyle. The day-trippers wear gangster suits and outlandish patterns and hats inappropriate to the latitude, temperature, or setting. It's amateur hour. They hold liquor like ninth graders. The homogenization of America has left people wandering the land in search of a place to belong. We are a tribeless nation hungry for tribes. That longing and loneliness are especially on display in early May in Kentucky.

From these seats, it felt possible to ignore all that change. Ignoring can be intoxicating. The view before us was the view people saw one hundred years ago. We couldn't make out the big battleship bridge behind us that dwarfed the spires. We only saw the flash of

the silks and the splashes of dirt and the blur of whip hands banging away for one more burst of speed. The race ended, and Julian
pulled a Cohiba out of his pocket and lit it. "My victory cigar," he
said. A grin flashed across his face. "I didn't bet on the race," he
said. "So I won."

- 2 -

MY NAME IS WRIGHT THOMPSON and I'm the writer. Julian and I originally sold this book as his story alone. That concept fell apart in the first trip when my own life kept mirroring and driving my conversations with the Van Winkle family. It was a strange time for me. The few days before arriving at the track had been full of nervous uncertainty. My wife and I were waiting on a phone call from our fertility doctor. My wife's name is Sonia and she's a writer and editor, too, with beautiful big brown eyes and wavy brown hair. She's smart, funny, with enough of her mother's Iowa farm girl can-do toughness that she moves through our lives like a miracle worker. But there was one miracle we just couldn't seem to work. There had been so many failed attempts to get pregnant. Finally we'd reached the end of the road. The doctor told us this was our last chance to have a family. There was nothing left to do but wait for the news and hope, so I decided to go ahead to Kentucky on my work trip. I felt myself spiraling. Never in my life did I remember feeling so tense and untethered, and I couldn't imagine how Sonia could manage knowing that this was either happening or not happening inside her own body. I expected the news a day or two after the Derby, and then the turmoil and worry would end either way. Normally that knowledge would bring a kind of peace: we'll get this news and then deal with it. But if I'm being honest, I didn't know if we could deal. I liked our life and feared that bad news might make going back to that life seem impossible.

Those were the stakes in my mind. Yes, I know that's a lot of confession right at the beginning, but I wanted to try to explain how the book came to be what it is. Julian and I are friends now, partly because of our visits but also partly because of the timing of those visits. Julian entered my world immediately after his successful battle with cancer, having confronted death, and I entered his while praying for a positive test result and thinking about life.

Sitting in the box seats at Churchill Downs, I watched Julian take a draw on his cigar and exhale into the humid Louisville air. The smell of the smoke reminded me of all the times I'd sat around as a child and watched the grown men and wondered when I might be like them. Julian looked out at the infield clock, counting the hours until the featured race.

- 3 -

WE HAD TIME TO PASS before the Kentucky Oaks, which is a mile and an eighth for three-year-old fillies held the day before the Derby. Oaks Day had long been my favorite racing afternoon of the year.

"The Derby is a shit-show," I said to Julian over the noise. "And the Oaks is just as fun."

He shook his head.

"This is just as crowded," he said. "Friday used to be the locals' favorite. Now it's pushed back to Thursday." So many tourists now come to the Oaks that the real local time at the track is Thursday—nicknamed Kentucky Thurby. I won some money yesterday, so I was loving the Thurby.

Sitting here on Oaks Day, I looked around and felt at home, like I'd discovered a long-lost family who had found me wandering and brought me back into the fold. The prodigal drinker returns. Julian is an archetype for the kind of man I'd like to be: a lover of fine wine and food, a traveler, a storyteller and court-holder, a good wing shot, a devoted father to one son and triplet daughters. Hanging around him requires being focused and funny—he is of a generation and social class that were taught how to play verbal ping-pong at rollicking dinner parties—and I always walk away feeling like I've gone back in time to sit with my father and his friends. Julian has an old jukebox in his basement, along with white dog moonshine off his grandfather's still at the Stitzel-Weller distillery the family owned until greed forced a sale. I'd learn a lot more about the trauma of that loss as I got to know Julian more in the coming years. It's the essential conflict of his life: something was built, something was lost, and he was left with the pieces.

Stitzel-Weller is considered by connoisseurs the finest bourbon ever made, smooth and complex. After the Van Winkle family lost the distillery in 1972, and it was sold, some new corporate owners changed the distilling process to save money and now that taste can never be re-created. Even the precious self-propagated yeast was abandoned in the name of progress. Powdered yeast is easier to manage and carries less risk of cross contamination, but while it always works, it doesn't have the same complexities. More and more today, we don't want to do the work or take the chances required for greatness, and we try to fix all those shortcuts on the back end with marketing and branding—modern, fancy words that mean lie. The old living yeast, Julian said, is still in some corporate freezer in New Jersey or somewhere, lost like the Ark of the Covenant at the end of *Raiders of the Lost Ark*.

The night before the Oaks, Julian took a bunch of his whiskey to a charity event in Lexington. The longer we spent together the more I saw him quietly using his supply of Pappy to help people. The charity sold three 10-year-old bottles, three 12s, two 15s, along with a 20, a 23, and one of the truly impossible to find 25-year-old decanters.

"How much all together?" I asked.

He said, "$178,000."

"Who bought it?"

"A car dealership guy in Lexington."

"Who gets the money?"

"Lexington Cancer Foundation."

We were walking through the grandstand toward the concession concourse. People stumbled around us all fucked up. I mean, shitrocked. The surest way to tell the people who had arrived here for an anachronistic weekend versus those who came every year was to look around and see who could hold their booze. Because everyone was drinking like they needed to forget some horrible thing they'd done. Some people rolled with it, and others . . . well, at that moment, I caught a falling drunk girl.

"Whoa!" Julian said, laughing. "Some of these people aren't going to make it through the day."

- 4 -

WE GOT TO KNOW EACH OTHER. I worked even on the first day to sort out what was authentically Julian and what I was projecting onto him. At the start, I saw him most clearly as the gatekeeper to a great bourbon whose roots give it a sense of permanence in an industry given over to fads and to marketing sold as tradition. He was careful never to speak ill in public of other whiskey makers but I had no such reservations. Julian never oversold his story to me, like, say, the folks who claim a family recipe for whiskey they buy in bulk from someone else. It's a line that was hard to hold and ever harder to see, especially for the customers, but one Julian walked with care.

That night after the races, he and I had a plan to drive out to a party at his family's old distillery. It's now home to Bulleit. Tommy Bulleit uses the old office that belonged to Julian's father and grandfather.

I wanted to go for the same reasons Julian did not.

He's an outwardly confident guy who still carries inside him a scar. He doesn't know Tommy Bulleit, who might be a lovely guy. But the idea of Tommy Bulleit's using the distillery the Van Winkle family built leaves Julian feeling hurt and angry. If he's being honest, he is worried that the further his family gets from that distillery, the more likely the same phoniness is to infect them, too. Maybe that's why Julian tells everyone he meets that he doesn't make whiskey while the Bulleit folks talk about their old family recipe, which was once made for them by a competitor that was owned by a Japanese beer company, which was owned by the same Japanese conglomerate that long ago made the Zero fighter airplane. The Zero killed a great many Americans in the Pacific and probably tried to kill Julian's father. All of that is to say that enemies can become friends—my wife's grandfather invited his German guards to their POW camp reunions—and the world can evolve and shrink, but for certain kinds of men, like my own grandfather who refused to buy Japanese cars, there always remains a scar that never goes away. For Julian, physical proximity to the Stitzel-Weller distillery is that kind of scar.

His modesty is a way to protect himself and his progeny against decadence and decline. He will not praise himself, but luckily other people in the bourbon world will do it for him. His connoisseurship is rooted in his lifetime of tasting bourbon, which would make him at the top of his profession if that were his only skill. It isn't. There's something more intentional and personal at work when he sits down to curate the barrels that eventually become Pappy Van

Winkle. He is not finding a technically perfect taste, which doesn't exist, or trying to use his sophisticated palate to put out a product that the focus groups and market research tell him will stun the critics and wow the customer. He is trying to sell a whiskey that tastes like the Stitzel-Weller that exists mostly now in his mind. He never lost that taste, even if his family lost the facility that made it.

That night at Stitzel-Weller, the new owners, international conglomerate Diageo, were launching a high-end bourbon with a big fancy dinner, cohosted by the Southern lifestyle magazine *Garden & Gun*. "Stitzel-Weller, baby," Julian said again, a bit more wistfully this time. "I hope I know the guy at the guardhouse. It'd be fun to see him. He worked for my dad. . . . It was like 1972, he was twentysomething. I actually worked with him as a teenager. He's been there forever. It'll be a crazy night."

"I just want to watch your face," I told him.

He smiled. "It will be tough for me to keep my mouth shut," he said.

- 5 -

KENTUCKY IS AT THE CENTER of the Van Winkle family mythology, and in the days before I met Julian at Churchill Downs, I drove around the horse farms and pastures east of Louisville. It's impossible to separate Julian from his home state. It's no coincidence that bourbon and thoroughbred racehorses come from the same place because both are made or broken long before anyone ever sees them. I rolled down the windows and let the big engine on my car roar and growl as I made the kind of aimless country laps that defined my high school summer days.

Exploring this part of Kentucky is one of my favorite drives in the world, following State Highway 1967 and Iron Works Pike, turning on narrow lanes built alongside short stone walls. Above me stretched a canopy of green leaves. The sun coming through the branches landed on the blacktop in dappled patches of light. My purpose wasn't completely aimless though. I'd driven here, over hill and dale, with a mission: to find the ruins of an old mansion, hidden from the road by pastures and oaks, which I've had described to me in such fanciful terms that I don't fully believe anything that dramatic could really be standing. A local horse lover told me which unmarked iron gate to approach, and when my car got close, the gate opened. The land is now owned by one of those powerful families who've long come and gone from the world of thoroughbred racing. This one made its money in the life insurance game. I'm a middle-aged man with elevated liver enzymes and high cholesterol, so I've had to consider dying as a real thing, and I find my immediate reaction is this strange desire to leave behind monuments to myself, whether they come in the form of a book about bourbon or in letters to friends and family. The monuments we erect—shouting into the wind that we were once alive and had hopes and dreams—often end up becoming a shrine to the fallacy and futility of that desire itself.

A man in a pickup truck eyed me suspiciously. The road cuts through manicured pastures and rises slightly, headed toward the interior of the property. Once upon a time, this land belonged to a business partner of the Hearst family, who made his millions during one of the many California gold rushes. As an old man, he built a mansion for a new bride, nearly fifty years his junior, and for twelve years, it hosted the kind of parties that will make the papers this week in Louisville; grand affairs, the mansion glowing like an ocean liner. He named it Green Hills after the view. Twelve years later, he died without a will and the land went to auction to be split into pieces. The guy who bought this part couldn't pay the stiff taxes on a mansion he couldn't afford to keep in the first place. So he tore it down. Most of it, that is.

I'm reminded of a drive through Tuscany with my friend Fred Marconi, who had picked me up at a train station so we could go watch Siena play Florence in soccer. Rows of trees lined the road, pine and cypress. Castle keeps rose from the hills. He drove past the exit of the stadium. There was a place he wanted to show me first.

"Our Little Big Horn," he said. Marconi's family has lived in Siena for at least five hundred years—the paper trail ran out before relatives did—and he is proud of his history. This wasn't some old man talking. He was a forty-two-year-old graffiti artist who plays bass in a rock band. He's got a Ramones tattoo. He baptized his three-year-old son on the 750th anniversary of the battle that took place on the peaceful field he was driving me to see. Changing lanes, he swerved in and out of game-day traffic, telling the story.

"This was one of the biggest battles in the Middle Ages," he said. "It was September fourth, 1260. Dante talked about this battle in *The Divine Comedy* and said it was a terrible day. The Sienese turned the Arbia River into a red river of blood. We actually exterminated the Florentine army."

After the battle, the city-state of Siena flourished. Work started on a cathedral, which would be the biggest in the world. Some businessmen founded a bank. The reign lasted almost three hundred years, then the Florentine army got its revenge, taking the town. The cathedral remains unfinished.

- 6 -

UP TO THE RIGHT, I saw a flash of white through the trees.

Then it came into view, like something on Marconi's Tuscan hilltop, the strangest thing: four Corinthian columns and the wide marble and stone entrance stairs, the only part of Green Hills that remains. It was stranded out here like *Ozymandias*, except instead of sand stretching to oblivion, it was green Kentucky bluegrass. I sat on the steps and let the silence swallow me as I tried to imagine this place lit on a Derby weekend and the sound of the band flowing from the house, filtering out into the night. Big flowing dresses and gentlemen in imported shirts and ribbon ties, and the underside of that world, too. I liked how I felt out by these columns and what the view made me consider, and how those ideas fit so cleanly into the way I was thinking about Pappy and the Van Winkles, and about me and my own family, too. These ruins are shocking and yet clarifying. America is such a young country. We haven't been through nearly the national life cycles of so many nations around the world. Other places have grown accustomed, even numb, to the way cultures rise and fall and then try to pick themselves back up again. Horse racing, like bourbon, makes these big ideas small enough to see. I can close my eyes and hear the parties. Imagine making a drive out here and seeing the lanterns hanging from the trees, and the house glowing in the distance, the sound of music audible first, then the faint murmur of dozens of conversations, and finally the liquid treble of clinking champagne flutes and double old-fashioned crystal. When I open my eyes, the party stops. I am here and the air is cold and there are four lonely columns where an entire world once stood—a world that, in the decadence and majesty of its apogee, must have seemed invincible.

EVERYWHERE AROUND THIS HILLTOP were warnings to the owners and trainers in Louisville this weekend who imagine they are making history. Domino, a famous stallion, was buried in a grave with a worn marker just on the side of the road. Domino only produced nineteen foals yet is in the pedigree of the greatest horses that ever lived: Secretariat, Seattle Slew, Affirmed, Assault, Bold Ruler, Whirlaway, War Admiral, Gallant Fox, Omaha, Native Dancer, American Pharoah. Of the thirteen horses to win the Triple Crown, nine have Domino in their family tree. Now he was forgotten on the side of a road.

I CHECKED MY MAP and pulled into one of the many smaller farms cut out of what used to be the grand Elmendorf Farm, where Green Hills glowed at night. In a small white office, a woman sat behind a small desk, the front door open to catch the breeze. I breathed in the sweet smell of freshly cut grass. Across from the office is the old Elmendorf cemetery. Fair Play and Mahubah, parents of the famed Man o' War, were buried beneath a statue.

Man o' War himself lived out his days nearby on Mt. Brilliant Farm. When Greg Goodman, heir to a Houston air-conditioning fortune, bought Mt. Brilliant, he found a collapsing barn on the property. Clearly visible on one of the stall doors, bleached by the sun, was the name of its former resident: Man o' War. He could not believe what he'd found, something not even his real estate agent had known. He owned the great champion's stallion barn! "It still makes the hair on my neck stand up," Goodman said. "It's Mount Vernon. . . . George Washington slept here."

The hidden history of Kentucky is everywhere, relics of the booms and busts of people who tried to grab a piece of that permanence only to have it slip through their fingers. Most of these farms are owned by someone who made a breathtaking amount of money doing something else. In the rush of their purchase, most never stopped to think that they were probably buying from someone who'd lost a similarly breathtaking fortune. Nearly every horse farm comes with the silent warning of the construction magnate who took on one project too many, the coal baron who couldn't survive his industry's decline, the industrialist family that burned through its inheritance. That's what has always struck me at the Triple Crown races in general and the Kentucky Derby in particular. Our national psyche is nakedly on display in the owners' boxes: the rich and nervous owners; the flavor-of-the-month celebrities in big hats; the ballplayers with cash in their pockets for the first time; the new-money families desperate to get something; the old-money families desperate to keep it. Pick almost any famous old horse and its farm and the story will be the same. Take Man o' War. The Goodman family owns his old home now and perhaps it will remain theirs for generations, or perhaps some tech billionaire will buy it if the air-conditioning money ever runs out. The current belles of the American economy are always on display in Kentucky, especially in May at Churchill Downs. Man o' War's barn was built by a wool mogul who had a horse in the Derby eighty years ago, racing against horses owned by the heir to the Mars candy fortune, a glass magnate, a gambler famous enough to be on the cover of *Time*, a paper magnate, a Texas ranching family whose descendants are *still* fighting over the land, and Marshall Field.

This year wasn't that much different. There were two oil and gas men, a pesticide executive, a chemical salesman, a high-interest mortgage lender once called a "loan shark" by the governor of California, a pro-hockey team owner and powerful Trump supporter, two investment bankers, and a cofounder of A&M Records. The whole thing, to be honest, is right on the line between ritual and campy reenactment. Horse ownership seems like a renaissance fair for millionaires. Churchill Downs is safe harbor in a world that didn't want them to have those fortunes and is always trying to take them away.

They all see themselves reflected in a great horse's eyes, which actually shine or glow with something primal, often mistakenly described with human emotions like fire and rage. Really it's a mystery, hundreds of years of breeding firing pistons on some unseen genetic engine that a few animals have and most do not. It seems like destiny, which is what the owners are really buying, for the animal and for themselves, but is often just luck. The fight to beat those odds is the bedrock of Kentucky. Its traditions and rituals, especially bourbon and racing, strive to push that knowledge out of sight. Man o' War is buried next to his most famous son, War Admiral, who won the Triple Crown but lost the famous match race to Seabiscuit. Seabiscuit's grave has been lost, at least its exact location; it's somewhere beneath a parking lot owned by a California religious cult.

Seattle Slew, who won the Triple Crown forty years ago, is buried at Hill 'n' Dale Farm near Lexington, which used to be owned by a construction mogul and is now owned by the son of a horse breeder. Hill 'n' Dale stallion manager Aidan O'Meara met me at the barn as he took the former champion Curlin out for some guests. One of the people asked whether Curlin was a kind horse, a question O'Meara tolerated with a smile. Thoroughbreds are the equine equivalent of pop stars—they're divas and brawlers, egomaniacs. But he knew racing fans like to project human qualities onto the animals. Horse people hate that. In some ways, the desire to make them pets takes away from their magnificence—the things about DNA and bloodlines we still don't understand; centuries of breeding to create the perfect running machine.

O'Meara recalled the day Seattle Slew arrived, struggling to recover from an operation, in the last two months of his life. "It was almost like a presidential motorcade," he said with his Irish accent, standing by Slew's old stall. "There was five cars in front and five behind the van. It was early, early morning. I can still see the cars coming up over that little hill, all the lights. He just came in as cool as you like. He strolled into that stall."

Six or seven weeks later, unable to recover from the operation, the horse died—on the twenty-fifth anniversary of his Kentucky Derby win. It was a day much like this one. O'Meara and his team pulled Seattle Slew out on a tarp. A man with a backhoe dug a grave and they tied the horse's legs together and lowered him into the ground.

Most horses have only their heart and hooves buried, but O'Meara and his team buried all of Seattle Slew: a sign of respect. He knows it's silly to get too emotionally attached to a horse he only knew for a few weeks, but that's how O'Meara felt that morning: like something powerful had left the earth. There was a brief yet tangible hole left by Seattle Slew's life force, the unknowable thing that made him so rare and coveted, a convergence of blood and genes that advanced analytics still haven't decoded. All these generations of boom and bust and all these billions of dollars made and spent to chase something that almost never arrives.

"I still remember," O'Meara said. "We lowered him down into the grave. I was holding his head. We had a blanket we put over him. People always talked about the fire in his eyes. I can still remember when we pulled the blanket over him, I looked into his eyes one last time. I still get chills talking about it. The fire was gone."

- 8 -

THAT FIRE OF BIRTH AND BLOOD is the most essential ingredient of many things that come from this part of the world—especially bourbon. It is more important than corn or wheat or water. The key to bourbon is time. Julian likes to talk about whether or not the whiskey put into the barrel to age "makes the trip." That is, will it emerge from that barrel as a fine bourbon or will something happen to it along the way? His whiskey hibernates for a long time, as long as twenty-five years, and once the barrel is stored in the warehouses, there's nothing Julian or anyone can do to guarantee that the magical living process is playing out as it should. Bottling doesn't promise survival, either. Just as time is the greatest ingredient in bourbon, it is also its greatest enemy. Time and air can destroy whiskey.

Once Julian and I went to a tasting together where some people had purchased these old bottles of his grandfather's whiskey, Old

Fitzgerald, made with the original Stitzel-Weller juice. They wanted him to talk about his family and to taste this booze. He took a sip and I could tell he didn't like it. Something had happened to the whiskey in that bottle. It hadn't made the trip. The romantic in him, in all of us, wanted some of his grandfather—some of a world now vanished—to exist inside that bottle. The critic in him knew it did not. But . . . sometimes it does. That's the magic. Sometimes the seal holds, and when you pour a glass and sip it—Julian likes his bourbon on the rocks with a twist—you have now traveled back a quarter century into the past, or further, depending on the age of the bottle.

The key difference between Old Fitzgerald and Pappy Van Winkle (and Weller and Maker's Mark and a few other high-end bourbons) is that the dominant secondary grain is wheat. Let's have a brief lesson about modern whiskey. There are strict guardrails for the grain, designed and pushed by powerful lobbyists who want to help their bosses maintain and protect market share. Bourbon, among its many codified restrictions, must be at least 51 percent corn. After that, though, the bourbon distiller has some discretion in picking the mix of secondary grains. Most use rye and barley. A few, like the Van Winkle brands, use wheat. That was made popular by Julian's grandfather. His biggest contribution to modern bourbon is that he was the first to make and sell a mass market fine whiskey with wheat as its dominant secondary grain.

The core ethos of the industry has long been to make something for a little and sell it for a lot.

One of the reasons the old-timers respect Pappy is that his motto, Always Fine Bourbon, wasn't just marketing. Stitzel-Weller put its white dog (the industry name for moonshine) in barrels at a lower proof than the maximum allowed by law, which cost the distillery money in taxes but made for better whiskey. Almost nobody does that today, because accountants and CFOs usually have more power than anyone who actually works a still or rolls around a barrel, and any issues with taste are just problems for the marketing team to fix.

Here's how it works.

There is a federal law that says bourbon cannot be put into a barrel at any proof higher than 125 (in the 1960s, the law said 110 proof, which is one of the reasons people rave about these older bourbons. . . . Turns out, your grandfather's whiskey really *was* better). The higher the proof of the booze going into the barrel, the more liquor there will be to sell once the aging process is finished. Same goes for the proof of the white dog off the still. Bourbon must come off the still at no higher than 160 proof, and the lower that number, the less complexity has been stripped out.

A few companies still put their liquor in the barrel at less than the maximum allowed proof, like Michter's at 103 and Maker's Mark at 110. That's rare, since most distilleries are run by accountants. When Pappy ran Stitzel-Weller, he got to overrule the accountants. Master distillers all know how to make a better product but often aren't allowed to do so. Pappy always staked his reputation on his independent company not cutting corners. It's why dusty bottles of Old Fitzgerald still command absurd prices on the secondary market.

But don't make Julian's granddad into some kind of saint; he was first and foremost a salesman.

He was the seller of romantic ideas, not the buyer of them. Turns out, wheat survives extended aging better than bourbons with rye as a secondary grain. Of course, that meant it was better at a younger age, too, which is likely what Pappy wanted. With Prohibition repealed the day before he started construction on the new Stitzel-Weller plant, there weren't huge supplies of aging whiskey sitting around, and Pappy needed to get whiskey out the door of his new distillery and into customers' hands as quickly as possible. He knew how to tell a story about himself and his whiskey. The reason Pappy's office was built to look like Monticello, with the leafy grounds of the Stitzel-Weller plant made to feel like an oasis from modern life, was because he knew that bourbon drinkers were often motivated by nostalgia—by this desire to stop the march of time and the cold hand of reality. It's a drink made for contemplating, and what is usually being contemplated is the easy and often false memory of better days. The bottle itself takes us there; it's why Mississippi Delta farmers still drink Old Charter, even though it's not nearly as good as it used to be, or why a Heaven Hill or Kentucky Tavern label reminds a lot of Southern boys of high school, or how the red wax on a Maker's Mark bottle evokes your father's liquor cabinet.

Opening a bottle of Pappy is a way for some people to signal they don't need to care about money, while for others it is a way to show a guest how much they are valued. When my friend, the great writer Charles P. Pierce, first came to my house to visit, I opened a bottle of Pappy 23. That was my way of saying: I am humbled and grateful for you to be in my home. A bottle of bourbon is a coded way for so many unspoken ideas to be transmitted and understood. In many ways, the most important ingredient in bourbon is added by the drinker once the bottle is purchased, which is why whiskey companies know to tell a story and stick to it.

Here's the story they don't want to tell: eight companies make 95 percent of the whiskey in America. When you walk into a liquor store and see all those labels, that's marketing. Templeton Rye and Bulleit Rye, for instance, have both been made by the Orwellian-sounding MGP, which is in Indiana, not Kentucky. Whiskey is better when it's mass produced by an expert and a team of chemists, not done in small artisanal batches by a guy who talks about craft. And all those different brand names are just that. Brands. Perhaps no word sums up the death of truth in America better than the word *brand*.

The term *brand name* comes from the whiskey business, according to Reid Mitenbuler, author of the excellent book *Bourbon Empire*. Nearly all pre-Prohibition whiskey was sold in barrels that were rolled into bars and tapped; the makers used a hot metal brand to sear their name into the top of the barrel so they could be identified. Mitenbuler's book explores many different threads, from how bourbon came to be associated with Kentucky to how it burrowed its way into our national consciousness. Mostly what he does, point by point, is strip away all the layers of myth and spin and bullshit. That Kentucky has become home to this industry is perfect, because it is a "colorful state with mythic origins, where history collides with mystery."

A lot of the famous brands, like Elijah Craig and Evan Williams, were created by Jewish distillers who presumed that their customers didn't want to open a bottle of Rosenstein Straight Bourbon Whiskey. The characters the distillers invented, the alleged fathers of bourbon, were ginned up mostly out of thin air, taking tiny threads of true biography and weaving a compelling fiction. The fine print on the back of bottles remains full of little lies. Look for words like *produced by* instead of *distilled by*, and don't bother to fact-check the histories told in gauzy, romantic language. But the opposite is true, too. They are selling you a lie you desperately want to be told. Mitenbuler writes: "Don't believe 90 percent of the tales you read on whiskey bottles but don't forget to enjoy them either."

So let's talk about what was on the Old Fitzgerald label and, more importantly, what was actually in the bottle. Stitzel-Weller bourbon was made from 72 percent corn, 20 percent wheat, and 8 percent barley. That's called a mash bill—the list of grains that get combined to create the mash that is the foundation for whiskey. The word *recipe* gets thrown around a lot and when the marketing people start talking about it, you need to get real suspicious real fast. Bourbon doesn't have a recipe. It has a mash bill.

Some people know Stitzel-Weller's mash bill and many others try to guess. A friend bought a copper still on the internet and hosted a party behind a big Mississippi mansion where he took those grains, in those percentages, and made it into white dog (aka moonshine) that everybody sat around firepits and drank. And while the idea of a recipe is intoxicating and fits into our view of bourbon as a rigorous craft, something akin to fine cooking or a birchbark canoe, that's misleading and a modern spin on a process that never really worked like that in practice. Precise and proprietary mash bills are a modern invention, something that happened to whiskey once marketers and salesmen and lobbyists got involved in what had been primarily a farmer's business.

I got to know the late moonshine runner and stock car legend Junior Johnson pretty well, and once I asked him for a mash bill and he sent it to me in old-fashioned and inexact measurements like pecks and bushels. I'll never forget the language he used, a new kind of postmodern grease poetry, when we sat in his shop and he talked about cars:

The 1944s had the same motors as they got now. Like a Cadillac, overhead valve, supercharged, bored out, stroked, cammed, and hell fire . . . you could run it. They said you can't get a Cadillac motor in a '44 Chevy. They just dropped right in there. Dropped it in a dad-blame frame and called Vic Edelbrock. Talked to him. Built me a manifold, three or four carburetors. Then they had that lawn mower people, made the McCulloch, they made a supercharger. Shit, I got me one of them things and adapted it. Had to build brackets and stuff. You hook that thing to that fan belt and it started whining, and when it started whining, you had some damn power. Sitting there with three carburetors and that's all I needed. You could put camshafters on that and hydraulic lifters on it and that thing would run so fast you couldn't even see the road. And that ain't no shit.

In the same way that Colonel Sanders wasn't a real colonel, the bluegrass bourbon business is an intentional creation, designed by salesmen who wanted to give the public a reason to buy their product and not someone else's. Kentucky, Mitenbuler writes, didn't have the monopoly on bourbon that it does today until after Prohibition, and that dominance was established by well-paid agents working on Capitol Hill and Madison Avenue.

American whiskey actually came into being when the first stirrings of manifest destiny took hold of the American imagination and people began to move west, first to Pennsylvania and then filtering out from there. New York and Pennsylvania rye farmers birthed this national tradition. They were farmers who wanted to stay on their land. The history of American whiskey is tied to that quest, all the way back to the first drop that rolled off the first still in the New World. It was a product, a crop, no different than cattle driven to slaughter or grain shipped to the coast. The earliest how-to books about making booze make it clear that the grains should always be whatever the farmer had easy access to, and that it's fine if the ratios, or even entire categories of grain, change from year to year. Whiskey is designed to be constantly evolving, to reflect the land from which it's made, and virtually all the current rules applied to its manufacture were designed by advertising wizards and businessmen eager to protect their share of the market.

For farmers, whiskey was the only way to get full value from their crops. Not everyone had access to markets and distribution methods, so to feed their family and keep their land, a man sought to do something with the surplus of a harvested crop. The dominant crop at the time was rye. They were spending time and money carefully planting and growing rye, and saw no point in watching that money rot before their eyes.

So they turned rye into whiskey.

What happened next would send ripples into the American future that we're still dealing with today: it began with a man who'd become the subject of a huge Broadway musical and ended with Jefferson's Republican Party replacing Washington's Federalist Party. The American Revolution earned the country its freedom but cost incredible amounts of money, most of it paid for by state-financed debt. Treasury Secretary Alexander Hamilton wanted the federal government to assume that debt and impose a sizable whiskey tax to help pay for it. He saw it as a sin tax, ignoring the economic realities of rural life that led to whiskey's distillation in the first place. It wasn't the first time a city dweller didn't understand life in a world different from his or her own.

George Washington, who made whiskey at Mount Vernon, knew different.

He opposed the tax at first, but a listening tour through Virginia and Pennsylvania in 1791 persuaded him. Congress passed the bill. And then, to use academic historian language, the farmers and distillers of Western Pennsylvania, the frontier at the time, went batshit crazy. This was the first bubbling of the Tea Party Movement, the anti-government strain that continues to exert great control over American politics. The new sin-tax law punished farmers who needed to make whiskey to maintain value, which meant that the farther away from the seats of power a man lived, the more likely he was to be hit by this tax. And the large distillers used their influence to keep the bill from crushing their businesses; they paid six cents per gallon and accrued substantial tax breaks. Small distillers paid nine cents per gallon.

The revolt that simmered and ultimately forced Washington to send in troops is now known as the Whiskey Rebellion. Until it was quelled, real fear existed that it could turn into a second revolution. Washington himself rode at the front of his army. Mitenbuler describes the Founding Father as tired and weary, with his steel dentures cutting into his gums. You can just see a haggard old man who wants to return to his farm, put down his guns, and age and rest and die in peace.

President Washington won the rebellion and strengthened the power of the federal government, but in the process the major debate in American public life was cemented, baked in, really. Nearly every political and cultural flashpoint we've experienced since is descended from this divide. Hamilton favored concrete and tall buildings and Wall Street, where he's buried, while Jefferson favored Main Street and the dirt of the rural America in which he's buried. Violence and discord over Hamilton versus Jefferson remain the greatest threats to the health of our experiment in democracy.

At the time of the Whiskey Rebellion, the Ohio River Valley produced the vast majority of America's whiskey, nearly all of it rye. Today, Kentucky produces the bulk of America's whiskey, nearly all of it bourbon. This switch seems random and complicated and yet it is actually quite simple. The farmers and distillers ran from the tax man and the long arm of the feds, looking for a piece of land where they might make their stand.

Hamilton's tax law passed in 1791.

Kentucky became a state in 1792.

In Kentucky, the land was perfect for corn—four times the yield per acre than Maryland, according to *Bourbon Empire*—and so the farmers naturally grew corn. The same laws of supply and demand that created whiskey followed the farmer-distillers from Pennsylvania to Kentucky. They faced the same existential challenges. Without modern supply chains, and because they were living on the edge of civilization, the farmers still couldn't monetize all of their crop before it rotted. So just as their forefathers did in Pennsylvania, they needed a way for their corn—and for their pigs—to hold value. Cured hams came from this need. And so did bourbon. Soon whiskey was traded as a currency, avoiding government notes and any taxes associated with them, which is why the IRS has long been obsessed with chasing down moonshiners and bootleggers. To Kentuckians, that is a federal war on working rural families, no matter what it's called in Washington. The spirit of modern Kentucky remains defined by its farmers. It might be called the Bluegrass State, but it just as easily might be the Corn and Wheat State. Many farmers have been growing grains here for eight or nine generations. A family farm in Loretto, now in its thirteenth generation, grows all the soft red winter wheat used in Maker's Mark. Distillers buy a lot of local grain. Each barrel of bourbon contains sixteen bushels of corn, and two thirds of the corn used for Kentucky bourbon is grown in Kentucky itself.

Here's what you won't see growing along a winding Kentucky road: rye, the traditional dominant grain in American whiskey and long the most popular secondary grain in bourbon. There's almost no rye grown in Kentucky. The amount is so small the US Department of Agriculture doesn't even track how much—less than 1 percent of total farmed acres. Rye is primarily a Northern crop and its inclusion in the mash bills of so many bourbons isn't because of geography but because of tradition and habit. But if whiskey is supposed to be a reflection of the land around the place where it's made, if it is going to carry with it some metaphysical power greater than the assemblage of molecules by PhDs in a lab, then it seems to me that it needs to carry its home with it out into the world. In Kentucky—and you can tell this by just going on a weekend drive—that means fields of corn and wheat, stretching out toward distant tree lines, not rye.

I'd always thought that wheated bourbon tastes smoother because wheat is softer than rye, and the chemistry is different, but now I wonder if the magic comes from a deeper place. The wheat makes the whiskey distinctively Kentuckian—a drink born after the rebellion and the diaspora south and produced from the grains that sway in the wind all around the distilleries. Bourbon made with rye is a holdover from Pennsylvania, from a tradition that traveled south. Instead of using the local grains, distillers have rye shipped in from Minnesota and the Dakotas and other states where it grows in abundance. On that Derby Day in 1935, Pappy Van Winkle stepped away from his competitors and released a different kind of bourbon into the market, one of this place—of *his* place. Fields of grain surrounded the distillery when Julian was a boy and Pappy was still alive. Corn, of course, and millet planted for the doves. On the weekends in September, the Van Winkles would go out in those fields and shoot doves. Even now, a half century later, Julian tells me, "I can still hear the shotgun blasts reverberating off the corrugated metal sides of the warehouses."

That's what Pappy was bottling and sending out across the world. Using wheat in bourbon wasn't his idea—it had been done by Weller in Kentucky and Charles Nelson in Tennessee—but he was the first to mass produce it. He was the first to become famous doing it, and that built his still vibrant legacy. He kept faith with the true idea of whiskey instead of stubborn traditions dictated by myth and custom. Each bottle of Old Fitz carried with it the God Spark of home. In those bottles, Pappy built a monument to his state, and to his family, and to himself. The wheat once and for all made bourbon truly *of* Kentucky. That was Pappy's triumph. He'd finally shaken the dominion of Pennsylvania out of the bottle.

- 9 -

IT WAS NEARLY TIME FOR JULIAN AND ME to leave Churchill Downs and go to the party. Safe under the grandstand, we looked out at the black clouds rolling in across the land. The weather had turned. The skies looked ready to open and attack, menacing. It was going to be duck boot weather. Julian had come prepared. I had not. We decided to make a break for my car, which was parked on the back side of the track near the barns. It would be a short ten-minute drive to the Stitzel-Weller distillery; easy once we made it to the car. We left the box and navigated the bowels of Churchill Downs. Walking beneath the covered concourse behind the grandstand, Julian filled me in on the latest strange internet trends to hit Pappyland: people were buying empty bottles online to fill with some other bourbon and then just pretend they're serving (or selling) Van Winkle. Not long ago, Julian got sent a counterfeit bottle, recapped by an industrial machine. When he tasted the fake

Pappy, he had to give the crooks a bit of credit: they'd used good whiskey in the scam, close enough to fool an average consumer but not close enough to fool Julian. We both just shook our heads and looked up at the sky. The rain held off and we skirted the edge of the track. The back side ahead of us was its own ecosystem, the domain of the hot-walkers and grooms and stable hands, most from Mexico and Guatemala, some of them undocumented, moving together in a crew from track to track and race meet to race meet.

"It's a wild scene back here," he said.

Finally safe in my car and moving, we waved at the guard at the stable gate and tried to escape the tangle of cars and trucks and flashing lights that clogged the small residential streets surrounding the racetrack. People were doing whatever they wanted. Some idiot was headed right for us.

"Oh, this guy's going the wrong way," Julian said. "Welcome to the Derby."

Julian gave directions: left on Fourth Street, left on Central Avenue. We passed the Wagner's Pharmacy, which had an old lunch counter where the horse folks gather. He talked on the phone to his son-in-law, Ed, married to his daughter Chenault.

"He's a good dude," Julian said when he hung up. "He's a master carpenter. If you need a mahogany library or wine cellar or whatever, he can do that. Now he's moved up here and Chenault has her own interior design company, and she was actually in *Southern Living* this month. She wanted to move home."

Julian said that Ed would be there tonight.

"He's a hunter, fisherman, a craftsman," Julian said, "and he's an Elvis impersonator."

I couldn't hide my surprise. Julian laughed. "At weddings, like friends' weddings, he's got a full-blown Elvis outfit," he said. "He had an old one but we got him a new one for Christmas. The premier Elvis outfit maker in the country is across the river in Jeffersonville, Indiana. So we went over there and got him a brand-new suit and it is amazing. It's got rhinestones and fits him perfectly. It's clean. It's not all ratty like the one he had."

"That's the most amazing gift I've ever heard."

"Well, he deserves it. He's amazing and he can play the guitar. He's got a wig and the glasses and he can sing. It's pretty funny."

The sun sank lower and lower, and we were headed toward a party with great food and whiskey and it was Derby weekend.

"How do you know you should be an Elvis impersonator?" I asked him.

"I guess he liked Elvis."

- 10 -

I WISHED I COULD RISE OUT OF THIS CAR and look down on Julian and myself as we moved west away from the weathered tan oval of the racetrack and toward the Indiana bluffs rising on the far side of the Ohio River, just a few miles away from Stitzel-Weller; the same river that brought those rye farmers south, looking for the freedom they thought they'd found in Pennsylvania. I'd like to see it all from above. "Go up in an airplane," Louisville's most famous son Muhammad Ali once said. "Go high enough and it's like we don't even exist. It's dust, all dust. Don't none of it mean nothing. It's all only dust." Kentucky used to be the edge of civilization, the great American frontier that would continue pushing west and give birth to all sorts of American myths: Little Big Horn, Route 66, Wounded Knee, rushes for land in Oklahoma and gold in California, *The Grapes of Wrath* and the Oregon Trail, let's go surfing now, everybody surfing now, look away down Gower Avenue. You can see all of the distilleries together from high enough in the clouds, and their lumbering rickhouses and brick chimneys blur and erase the idea of time and history, pressing them together into one American dimension: the farming past, the marketing present, and a future that offers the possibility that our best days are ahead or have already peaked, running on the fumes of whatever national spirit sent us first to Kentucky and then on to California in wagons, in cars, on planes, on fiber-optic cables buried beneath the farms and buffalo plains.

All these famous distilleries can be visited in two or three days: Stitzel-Weller to Maker's Mark and Jim Beam and Willett to Buffalo Trace to Woodford Reserve to Four Roses and Wild Turkey. Bulleit's marketing wizards call it frontier whiskey, which seems strange if you imagine the frontier as the backdrop for *Dances with Wolves*, but that's really what bourbon is and what it evokes for so many: a past that might not be true but sure seems better than whatever present we're living in. Maybe that's why bourbon is booming. Whatever the reason, the bourbon explosion that created the fierce demand for Julian's whiskey has also created a secondary market for "vintage spirits," for the old bourbons that don't get made any longer, and at the top of most collectors' lists are bottles made at Stitzel-Weller by Julian's grandfather and his father. The star of that world remains Old Fitzgerald, S-W's flagship brand. Those bottles go for exorbitant prices on the secondary market, a modern side effect of the whiskey boom that constantly brings drama to Julian's door: the prices people pay for his bourbon are not the prices he himself gets paid for them, which means he doesn't make anything and lots of people blame him for being gouged. But as the internet taketh away, it giveth, too: for a few years, until Sissy demanded he stop, Julian would stay up late online and buy these old bottles of Old Fitz, which can go for as much as $15,000— chasing something just like people chase Pappy Van Winkle— because he wanted to hoard as much of that vanishing taste as he could. He's got a storage facility full of these bottles to ensure he's always able to get that taste of his youth.

I love the image in my head of Julian at his computer, a few drinks deep into a melancholy nostalgia buzz—"crying about your daddy drunk," as the writer Dan Jenkins said—seeking out these bottle auctions. He's looking for dates that mean one thing to whiskey collectors but something much more personal to him, because they mark time in the passage of his life, and in his father's and grandfather's lives before him. He's got a lot of old, valuable bottles collecting dust. One afternoon, Julian brought out one of the rarest whiskeys in the world, the original Pappy Van Winkle that set the bourbon world on fire, and he sat it on his kitchen island.

"There are probably only five bottles of that left on earth," he said.

"We're not opening it!" I insisted. "I would feel terrible."

"Yeah," he said, "I guess I better give that to my children. Or I'll drink that when I'm in the nursing home. I'll call you."

When I started working on this book I bought a bottle of vintage Old Fitzgerald. Research. It sat in my bar waiting for the right time. I needed a reason to crack it open. Then a few years ago, Ole

Miss, the team that I support and that my father supported before me, played in the Sugar Bowl on New Year's Day. It was the first time the Rebels had made a Sugar Bowl since my father was a junior in college. We did our usual New Year's Eve dinner at the City Grocery in Oxford, Mississippi, and then we went to the airport and boarded a small plane to make the midnight run to New Orleans. I brought along a bottle of 1978 Old Fitzgerald and we drank it the whole way down. That's how we acknowledged the ghosts who'd be at that game with us. That's how we toasted them while we flew.

The whiskey was twelve years old, barreled in 1966—before I was born, before my parents ever met, back when my father was still a young man, his life still made of dreams. My dad was a freshman in college the year the Stitzel-Weller men ran corn and wheat and water through their still and then loaded it into barrels to age. Some piece of 1966 existed in the bottle, and in our glasses and on our tongues—inside of us—while the plane bumped and hopped through the air on the way south. As we landed, glasses in hand, the midnight New Year's Eve fireworks lit up the sky as we made our final approach into New Orleans Lakefront Airport. The magic of those exploding starburst shells, and knowing we'd be watching a game my father didn't live long enough to see, burned the images deep into my memory. I won't ever forget them. I believe that's why we covet bourbon so much. That is its great gift to us. It allows us to see clearly through dimensions, as long as we don't abuse it, because then it fucks up our lives and the lives of everyone who loves us.

Ole Miss won that game, and as our group walked away from the Superdome, we passed a restaurant and heard banging on the glass. I turned and saw a big group of my family sitting at a long table, celebrating the win. The first face that came into focus belonged to my uncle Will, the second of the four Thompson boys and my dad's beloved older brother. He's got one of those smiles. Some people's voices remain in your memory, or the way they walk, or a gesture. For Uncle Will, it's his smile. He waved me inside the restaurant. I hadn't known they were coming but I wasn't surprised, and a little part of me believed that they had been summoned by that bottle, that we had been brought together in communion. We embraced and toasted the Rebels and those of us who love them and those who loved them and had died. Uncle Will and I held eye contact for just a moment longer than customary, and a supercomputer of information passed between us in those long seconds. A century of people and places, faded but alive, suddenly became as real to me in that restaurant as any of the living, he and my dad in the bedroom where all four boys lived, or driving the Chevy Super-Sport they shared in college, or having babies and raising families, or my dad going in for a checkup and leaving with a death sentence, or he and Uncle Will during their final visit with each other. I wasn't there but I bet they prayed together, knowing that they would see each other again, in another place and world.

- 11 -

JULIAN AND I DROVE to the outskirts of town. We were less than a mile now from the distillery where he grew up, a boy king, son and grandson of the company president. Some of his earliest memories are from these shaded acres but until a few months ago, his children had never visited, not even once.

"When was the last time you were out here?" I asked.

He looked around.

"I haven't been on this stretch of this road for a long time," he said.

"Isn't that strange?" I asked him.

"Right, right," he said, quiet and curt, suddenly very far away.

"What did your kids want to see?"

"They just wanted to see the old office building and the look and the feel of the place and kind of learn a little bit about it," he said.

"It's funny what Diageo has done to it, it's full of experience, the tour, and the Blade and Bow thing."

"What's Blade and Bow?"

"Oh, it's their new brand," he said.

Diageo is capitalizing on the cultlike following that Stitzel-Weller now has in the bourbon world. That's a dramatic shift in strategy. After acquiring the distillery the company stopped using Pappy's yeast and got rid of all the machinery. The old-fashioned rollers and grinders weren't the most efficient machines but they added complexity and depth in ways nobody really understood until they were retired. Diageo used the Stitzel-Weller warehouses to age booze but abandoned the rest of the facility to rot on the outskirts of town. And even though the company stopped making whiskey like Julian's dad and granddad made, and then stopped using the plant altogether, there were all these barrels of the old Stitzel-Weller left over. They eventually became the most valuable and sought-after things in all of the bourbon world. But before the boom, most of those old Stitzel-Weller barrels got shipped by Diageo to Canada, where they became a tiny percentage of the Crown Royal blend. Diageo threw away hundreds of millions of dollars, although nobody realized it at the time.

"It's like the accountants take over the whole business," Julian said. "'Why don't we just use this existing shit that's in Kentucky?'"

The modern bourbon boom is built largely on Julian's grandfather and on the Stitzel-Weller bourbon that survived the spirit's time in the wilderness—when it was wasted on Crown Royal, for instance—and on replicating the connoisseurship and mythology of Pappy. It was a blueprint, and the industry followed it with enthusiasm and with a savvy understanding about who was buying their product and, more important, why. Julian has risen to the top of this boom because he's a five-tool bourbon player: he's got the most famous last name in a brand-obsessed world; he has a whiskey built on the famed and scarce Stitzel-Weller juice; and he has an organic connection to his juice, which seems unremarkable but is quite rare; and while those three would be enough to carve out a living, he's also got his grandfather's connoisseurship and is a living extension of his mythology. His family might have lost the distillery but Julian still has his inherited palate and his memory of how he believes great whiskey is supposed to taste. Lots of people are searching for the taste his family made famous, or at least hoping to draft in the Van Winkles' success.

"That's what this Blade and Bow is," Julian said. "They've got this Solara process. Have you ever heard of this? It's where you take some whiskey of a certain age and you take some of that barrel and put it in with some other barrels of different distillation; blend it with those. There might be a tiny piece of what was made at Stitzel-Weller that they kept, which they closed in '92, so it would be pretty old at this point."

Only a few turns remained. I made a left onto Ralph Avenue. We could see the old barrelhouses peeking up into the sky. I pulled up to Stitzel-Weller, turning onto Limestone Lane past the ivy-covered stone pillars he saw so often growing up. The hulking gray barrel-houses looked like a fleet at anchor. The replacement plaque with his grandfather's company motto is there: WE MAKE FINE BOUR-BON AT A PROFIT IF WE CAN, AT A LOSS IF WE MUST, BUT ALWAYS FINE BOURBON.

- 12 -

JULIAN HAD BEEN FEELING NOSTALGIC, which I only recently learned comes from the Greek words for *home* and *pain*. That seems about right. Home and pain. He was acutely aware that he was not immortal, no matter what working in an industry built on imagining a distant future tried to tell him. Maybe that was why he had been thinking a lot about his old 1966 pale-yellow Mustang with wire wheels and a black vinyl top and a black leather interior. Actually, it was his sister's car first and he just inherited it. He always showered at the distillery in the workers' locker room. That way he wouldn't get the seats dirty. His family got a deal on Mustangs because his dad bought a fleet of them for his salesmen from a local dealer. They were all white. But his was yellow, and it sat low to the ground and made a noise he loved, one he's still chasing: his current car is an Audi.

He loved that Mustang.

"I flipped it," he said.

He laughs.

There was a passenger in the front seat, his girlfriend at the time, a woman by the name of Frances. They were driving a winding road in Boyle County, following some friends to a roadhouse restaurant. A cooler of beer sat in the back. That's the gun on the mantel.

Julian pressed down on the gas, letting the throaty engine shake in its mountings, and as he topped a hill he found himself confronted with a hard-left turn he had not anticipated. Julian lost control and the Mustang slid off the road. The back end of the car got loose and he went into a ditch, the car rolling down the embankment until it landed upright on top of a tree stump. Julian was wearing his seat belt. Frances was not.

Julian collected himself and turned to check on his date. The passenger seat, previously occupied by the lovely Ms. Frances, was empty. He turned around and found her perfectly healthy and mightily annoyed, sprawling in the back seat, surrounded by an empty cooler and a lot of full cans of beer. The ice and water that had previously joined that cooler with those beers had been redeposited all over Frances's perfectly coiffed and sculpted bouffant, which now slumped in dejection.

"Totally drenched with ice water," he said.

Julian got out and saw that the stump upon which his Mustang had come to rest had, in fact, smashed the engine of the car. The car was fucked. After taking off the "Rebel Yell" bourbon license plate on the front, he got it towed. Julian ended up selling the wreck for about one hundred dollars. In the years that followed, he thought about that car a lot, and about the young man who whipped it up and down the hills of Kentucky, and in some of his darker moments, he wondered what had happened to both. Not long ago, he started looking for another one, a 1966 pale-yellow with the black interior and the black top. Soon friends joined in the quest. A restaurant owner in northern Kentucky who'd heard him talking about this quest came across one online and sent the link to Julian. The car was in Minneapolis and Julian bought it.

"You're deep in the nostalgia now," I told him.

"You get older, you got nothing left," he said.

When the pale-yellow Mustang arrived, he knew what to do. In his collection of odd stuff he's accumulated over the years, he found an old tin Rebel Yell license plate. He got model-airplane paint and carefully began restoring it—"the only time I've ever seen him do an art project," Sissy said, laughing—and when it looked perfect, which is to say exactly how it looked in the 1960s when everything was right in his family's distilling empire, he screwed it into place on the front of the car.

- 13 -

WE PULLED UP TO THE GATE at Stitzel-Weller. The past was all
around Julian now. Being here triggered so many thoughts, including the memory of how his family's old whiskey tasted and smelled.
His sister cried when she came back as an adult, seeing someone
else inhabiting her childhood memories. Julian's attachment is to
the place as well, but also to the taste. He has spent his adult life
chasing it. The past few years of his life have been dominated by a
long wait to reclaim that taste. Julian's great gift was always his
ability to taste new whiskey and predict how it might taste when it
aged, or to taste barrels and figure out how to blend them so they
might closely approximate the taste of the old Stitzel-Weller he
loved so much. In the coming months, he will taste the Buffalo
Trace made and aged as Pappy Van Winkle for the first time since
he partnered with them to ensure that his label would have a long
life even after he died. He hopes that this whiskey will taste

something like the Stitzel-Weller that made Pappy famous and rare, but there's no way to know if it made the trip. He has bet a lot on this particular tasting in this particular year.

The man working the Stitzel-Weller guardhouse for the party was Carroll Perry, a Vietnam vet who started work here after he returned from the war. Perry was still here. A long time ago, during those hot summers working in the warehouses, he nicknamed Julian "Ripper."

"Oh," Julian said, smiling warmly. "I was hoping I would see you."

"Nice to see you, sir," Perry said. "I remember your daddy. Yeah, Ripper Van Winkle. You know what got that started?"

"I'm afraid to ask," Julian said.

"It was in the warehouse break room," Perry said. "And you went back there and got a case of export and was handing out the little miniatures to all of us, and we was sittin' there when your daddy walked in. You got hell."

"I don't remember that part," Julian said. "I think I blocked that out."

"After that we called you Ripper Van Winkle."

"Well, it stuck. Will you be around tonight for a while?"

"Yes, sir. Until closing time. It's good to see you."

The white tent glowed like something pitched by Victorian gentleman hunters. Sets of couches formed nooks for talking. Long tables were set for the dinner by a famous chef. Dinner would include his riff on the KFC mashed potatoes, served alongside mutton saddle and a tuned-up Derby pie. Music played and bartenders manned stations all around the place. Julian and I ordered mint juleps.

"I've been avoiding them all day," he said.

"There's good reason to at the track," the bartender said. "How was your day?"

"I won a little money and then I quit betting," Julian said. "Can you believe that? I finally learned that's what you do."

The whole experience was weird for me to watch, like he was walking through some alternate version of his own life, not fifty paces from the main office where his father and grandfather had worked—where he and his father struggled to know each other, separated by generations and joined by the shoes they both felt pressure to fill. With the Van Winkles, it always somehow came back to Pappy and the legacy he created and still inhabited from the other side.

- 14 -

JULIAN PROCTOR "PAPPY" VAN WINKLE SR. opened his distillery on Derby Day in 1935, planted in boxwood and magnolia trees and set on a fifty-three-acre tract of land just outside the city limits to avoid the taxes. Construction started the day after Prohibition ended, two years earlier. He oversaw every detail, including the installation of the largest still in the world at that time, capable of producing a barrel of bourbon every 4.17 seconds. Fourteen years later a new brick office opened, with white columns and a Monticello-inspired rotunda over the porch. Instead of a knocker on the white door, they hung five brass keys, each representative of one of the five stages of bourbon: grains, yeast, fermentation, distillation, aging. "Fine bourbon ought to make itself," he liked to tell visitors, "with just a little help from mother nature and father time."

Pappy Van Winkle often got his picture taken out on the front steps, alone and with his son, or with his partners, or with whoever might stop by to see him. He and those white columns became intertwined, in the public's imagination and in the memories of his children and grandchildren. Pappy's brick office was the center of his world. It was where he ate a frankfurter without a bun and an onion sandwich for lunch and then napped on his big tan sofa. His office was where he built fires in the winter and looked through its windows at the magnolias and the grain fields. It was where he would hunt relentlessly when the weather warmed, shooting dove and quail. He kept his gear in an office closet that smelled of leather and gun oil. Dead birds ended up on tables around the place for him to take home at the end of the day for his wife to cook. The family's bird dogs lived in a pen next to the cooper shop: Pat, King, Thunder, and Chief. Julian and his sisters, Sally and Kitty, would often come and play with those dogs, running free in the groves and fields.

Julian saw the old shop where his granddad's hunting dogs had lived. That was where he first understood that what they did here was a craft. "My aha moment," he said. "I was working at the cooper shop. You dump the barrels in this trough, and roll the barrels down, take them apart, take the bad stave out, put the good stave in its place, put the cattails in between the staves. I learned how to do all that stuff; that was one of my jobs one summer. It was hard as hell. You put the barrel once it's fixed back under the hose in the trough up here and you open the knob, and you fill the barrel back up. Well, one time the hose didn't hit the hole right and I was completely soaked in that whiskey. And I tasted it, and that's when I went, 'Damn, this is really good.' It wasn't like sitting in a bar or sitting at home drinking whiskey, it was getting a bath in it. I was sixteen, seventeen, and I could tell how good it was. Once you taste that flavor, you never forget it."

That flavor was Pappy's life's work. Not the buildings or the business. Those were mere instruments. He made and sold a luxury product, refined instead of rough, more popular in private clubs than in roadside saloons. This wasn't cowboy booze, slamming a dirty glass down on a bar.

Pappy was an oddity in the Kentucky distilling world; he built himself up in this business from scratch, in a time and industry when nearly every other bourbon maker was from a long familial line, handed power and success by birth instead of work and luck. Pappy first got his start in whiskey at nineteen, when he took a job for W. L. Weller & Sons. It was 1893. He ended up buying out the Weller family and eventually merged with the Stitzels, who got their start when three German brothers moved to Kentucky in 1859, exactly a decade after the Wellers began making whiskey.

Pappy carried his outsider spirit with him his whole life. During a time when all the small producers were being swallowed by large corporations—most of the bourbon world was run by four large producers—he refused to let Stitzel-Weller be eaten. He testified before Congress in 1952 about the state of his industry, which was marred by price-fixing scandals and the general (and correct) assumption that there was more than a hint of organized crime involved in keeping America properly buzzed. "I think it's often overlooked how big of a juggernaut Pappy was," said bourbon writer and historian Fred Minnick, who has written some of the most deeply researched work on the spirit. "He took on the big guys. He looked down the barrel at the mob."

Pappy launched an armada of salesmen out into the world, and he treated those men like family, probably because he remembered when he'd been out on the road, trying to build something approaching the life he fully realized by the mid-1950s. Old Fitzgerald was the only brand that was always 100 proof. He never watered down his liquor to take advantage of a bourbon boom. Pappy held the line. That should be on his tombstone, along with the many sayings that Julian and his sisters still remember.

"I see no sense in shipping water all the way around the country."

"I used to be a Democrat but I soon got tired of that."

"If I wanted to drink vodka, I'd find someone who'd sell me a can of alcohol."

He lived the life of a country squire, bird hunting at work and training his dog Thunder to haul around his golf clubs at the Louisville Country Club. Whenever the dog arrived at the course, it leaped out and ran to the caddie shack to be outfitted for work. An acrylic painting of Pappy and Thunder on No. 18 hangs in Julian and Sissy's kitchen, and sometimes when Julian passes it at night, he'll smile and say, almost to himself, "There's Pappy and Thunder."

Pappy ruled this world until 1964 when he handed it over to Julian's dad. It was *his* company now. His burden and responsibility.

"In succeeding my father," Van Winkle Jr. told *Wine and Spirits* magazine, "I realize I must attempt to fill the shoes of a man who has become a legend in his own time and, in fact, an institution in our industry." Bourbon sales were declining around the country and the accountants pressed in on him. Pappy created the rise, and his son, facing forces beyond his control, would oversee the fall. That was his duty. So far the company had kept its flagship brand, Old Fitzgerald, at 100 proof, but a week after Julian's dad took over, he put an Old Fitz on the market at a watered-down 86.8 proof. It's clear the decision had already been made: Julian's dad saved his own father the indignity of finally caving after an entire career built on holding the line no matter the cost. Julian Jr. took on that shame so that his beloved father wouldn't have to take it on himself. When Julian's grandfather, Pappy, died on February 16, 1965, at 11:10 p.m., Julian's father stopped the clocks in his home.

Julian's father was soon fighting to survive an eroding business and family politics. He and his sister split Pappy's 51 percent stake, which is where the trouble began. The family who owned the 49 percent wanted more profit, and they were able to convince Julian Jr.'s sister that she deserved a higher return on investment, too, and that the whiskey business would never recover from its spiral. They brokered a sale with Somerset out of New York—owners of the Johnnie Walker and Tanqueray brands—which helped solve one of the conglomerate's problems. Somerset already owned a Kentucky distillery with lots of barrels of mediocre whiskey but it didn't have a brand to sell it with. So it wanted to water down the Stitzel-Weller's juice with all this subpar stuff just sitting there taking up room and costing the company money—using Pappy's reputation to sell shitty whiskey is how the Van Winkles simplify the business calculations. Julian's dad fought that sale off for as long as he could to protect the family's reputation for "always fine bourbon," but the tension caused by his efforts fractured the family. His sister basically wouldn't speak to him, and for the first time in his life, he gave up.

He stopped opposing the sale and on June 30, 1972, just seven years after Pappy's death, the Van Winkle family sold Stitzel-Weller to Norton Simon. Julian's dad left all the artifacts in the glass cases around the office, feeling that the history of the place should be transferred along with the property. But the new owners came in, emptied out those glass cases, and threw all of that stuff away or put it up for auction. One day his dad's former secretary, who'd stayed on with the new company, called them. She spoke in a whisper and told them there was an auction scheduled. The Van Winkle family treasures were being sold to the highest bidder and nobody had told them. Out of guilt and loyalty, she broke ranks to let them know.

They drove to the auction house. Julian and Sissy both remember a blizzard. There was one piece they wanted: a massive sterling silver punch bowl that came with a tray and a large set of cups, each engraved with the name of the top salesman for a particular year. The bowl, filled with eggnog, and cups would be brought out at the annual Christmas party, as the new stars of the whiskey-selling world were celebrated along with all the stars from the past. It was always a beautiful, moving evening and Julian wanted the bowl and the cups. A plant in the crowd designed to drive up the prices was bidding on everything, and when the bowl came up for sale, he bid on that, too. He and Julian were the only two people bidding and the price spiraled higher and higher until finally Sissy shot him a look, and he folded under her withering stare. The gavel came down, and for $5,000 Julian had his heirloom back. The Van Winkles still use the bowl and cups for Christmas parties.

Those are the memories that fuel his feelings of anger and resentment when he gets anywhere near the Stitzel-Weller distillery. It feels like a graveyard to him. That's how it is sometimes. A world is vibrant and feels eternal, so the little decorations of life don't mean much and are treated with passive contempt. Then that world is suddenly destroyed and the few remaining pieces are guarded and treasured. Even the plant's name got changed from Stitzel-Weller to Old Fitzgerald.

I remember sitting with Julian at his kitchen island in Louisville one afternoon, looking out on the backyard where he learned to drive. He grew up in the house next door. A rare bottle of whiskey sat on the counter and he picked it up and turned it around in his hands to read the label: Van Winkle Family Reserve. Bottled December 1984. Barreled November 21, 1968. When he opened the bottle, the whiskey smelled complex and looked almost viscous, thick with caramels and burnt oak. This was Stitzel-Weller bourbon, made three years after Pappy died and four years before Julian's dad lost the distillery. The smell filled the kitchen. He walked over to a drawer and came back with a razor-sharp French bar knife, then took a lemon and cut off two strips of rind and rimmed the glasses. He poured us each a drink, on the rocks, with a tiny bit of water to open up the flavor, and the twist.

He grinned after the first sip.

Sissy came in, carrying an old humidor. It belonged to his grandfather. An engraved brass plaque read:

Julian P Van Winkle Sr
Pappy
MARCH 22, 1963

I picked up the bottle we were drinking and found the date it had been distilled.

"Where were you on November 21, 1968?" I asked him.

Julian sat in his kitchen and let himself go back, doing math. He figured he must have been at the Blue Ridge School, his second boarding school after failing at the one where his dad sat on the board. "I was at Blue Ridge School, stealing horses, riding around in the mountains," he said. "My roommate and I, who was from Louisville, stayed at Blue Ridge for Thanksgiving. We broke in the tack shop and tack room and saddled up some horses and went riding around the Blue Ridge Mountains. And we almost got kicked out of school because when we brought the horses back I guess we left the food bin open. Horses are not as smart as mules 'cause they'll eat themselves to death whereas mules stop. And they almost died. So we almost got kicked out of school."

The old bottle had conjured all the spirits. Julian took a sip and sighed. He seemed melancholy. I asked him how he felt about selling whiskey when he knows the best whiskey that will ever exist was made by Stitzel-Weller and all he can hope for is to come close.

"I've fought with that my whole life," he said.

Close is always the only possible outcome when someone tries to make the present match up with his memory of the past. Home always seems warmer and safer than it really was. That's where the pain comes from. We long for a fantasy that won't ever come true and feel surprise at our inability to create it from force of will. That's what Thomas Wolfe meant, I think. We can't go home again because the home we remember never existed. All those ideas mixed with the ice to make the cocktail we really wanted. I asked Julian what the whiskey in his glass made him remember. He was sitting in his kitchen but was also very far away. He sighed again and told me that the taste always took him back to that long ago summer, the same year the bottle we were drinking was made, when he got soaked in Stitzel-Weller and fell in love with it. That was his baptism; he left that cooper shop changed, and so whenever he was back at the old distillery, part of him always returned to the summer of 1968. Or got as close to it as he could. He never got closer than close.

- 15 -

TIME STOPPED FOR HIM when he entered the gates on Limestone Lane. As he wandered, in a bit of a daze, I sipped on my free taste of bourbon offered by our hosts for the evening. Julian wouldn't like me saying it—and Sissy expressly warned us not to start any shit tonight—but the Blade and Bow wasn't great. I mean, I didn't love it. I mean, it tasted fine, is awesome in a Manhattan I bet, and by the third drink it didn't matter all that much. But the best whiskey in this entire place was in Julian's pocket. Always fine bourbon—made right on the premises before this was a museum, before the accountants shut it down.

"You didn't bring a flask in here, did you?" someone asked him.

Julian grinned, his eyes twinkling with his tiny act of rebellion.

"What do you think?" he shot back.

The whiskey lovers in the crowd cornered him to see what might be gleaned from an audience with Booze Yoda. I've spent a lot of time watching how people talk to him in person and online. He catches a ton of shit on the internet from fringe whiskey nerds who talk about his whiskey being overrated, or about how the scarcity is just a marketing plot, and online those attacks get personal. I've been with Julian when he was surrounded by whiskey nerds and nobody ever says that shit to his face. Some of these folks seeking an audience have no doubt attacked him online, but without the cover of anonymity their courage slips away. He poses for a lot of selfies and answers a lot of questions, which he actually seems to like, or at least tolerate. He can seem effusive enough to obscure just how private he really is.

"What do you carry in your flask?" an acolyte asked.

"Weller, it's all I can get," he said. "It's all the same recipe as our whiskey just a younger version, so it's like young Van Winkle whiskey. It's the same recipe as ours, originally made here."

When prompted, he explained the history of this place. He gestured to the buildings sitting in darkness outside the tent. "Did you know this was an old Pappy distillery? Stitzel-Weller. They started in 1935 back here. It's a corn, wheat, and malted-barley recipe versus corn and rye. All the wheated-recipe bourbons that are out there come from my grandfather, because Fitzgerald distilled Rebel Yell even though it's owned by Luxco in St. Louis. Old Fitzgerald is owned by Heaven Hill. Buffalo Trace owns Weller. Now for our purpose that's where most of our whiskey is made."

"How do you feel about Blade and Bow?" someone asked.

"Well, it's made in a different distillery," he said. "Diageo closed this in '92 and went with the new Bernheim whiskey distillery, which is now owned by Heaven Hill down the road. Different equipment equals a different flavor profile completely."

- 16 -

LET'S GET GRANULAR. Diageo is the current name of the owners of Stitzel-Weller. It owns Guinness among many other iconic brands. Under the name United Distillers, before a merger created Diageo, executives shut down the famed Stitzel-Weller plant in 1992 and opened a new distillery at Bernheim, which some consider the worst new distillery ever built. After it shut down the facility Pappy built, Diageo sold off nearly all the bourbon brands, although it still used the Stitzel-Weller warehouses for aging. When the bourbon boom started four or five years later, Diageo pulled the I. W. Harper brand out of mothballs and bought Tommy Bulleit's label. Diageo owned the Bernheim distillery and had access to juice. So people like bourbon historian and journalist Fred Minnick wonder whether the booze used in Blade and Bow is actually leftover juice made by Stitzel-Weller or whether it is Bernheim that was aged at the old Stitzel-Weller distillery. It's a subtle distinction, and one that doesn't matter to most folks but matters tremendously to bourbon obsessives.

Often an essential trait needed to sell bourbon is the ability to artfully dodge a direct question about what's in the bottle and how it got there. Not long ago I was on a tour at a famous distillery that shall remain nameless, and the guide said that one of its high-end offerings wasn't called bourbon because it was aged in special barrels that didn't match the strict government controls defining bourbon. I asked if the liquid in the barrel was all straight bourbon whiskey or if it had been cut with neutral grain spirits. She bobbed and weaved and didn't answer the question. Bourbon has always been a little about waving one hand wildly to attract attention away from what the other hand is doing.

Everyone with a connection to Pappy is trying as best as they can to sell that story. Stitzel-Weller talks about Pappy in its tour. Heaven Hill bought Old Fitzgerald and name-checks Pappy on its website. Weller, which is owned by the same people who now work in partnership with Julian at Buffalo Trace, is made from the same juice as Pappy—just not aged as long and not curated by Julian. Weller has become impossible to find just because of its association with Pappy. But in the end, the only real connection with Pappy and with Stitzel-Weller lives inside Julian himself. He remembers how the whiskey tastes and matching his memory remains the cornerstone of his process. "Julian's great gift is his palate," Minnick said. "You won't find many people with a better palate than Julian. He has this unique ability. That's not something you can teach. It's a straight-up gift."

- 17 -

JULIAN STOOD IN THE TENT and everything about him signaled that here was a man around whom others tended to revolve. He doesn't orbit. People orbit him. He sipped from the flask. The Weller had that same smoothness that is familiar to wheat lovers and was made from the same juice as Pappy. "That's why you can't find it," Julian said. "On account of people calling it Baby Pappy. That's why you don't really see Weller much."

"So what's the difference between their Weller and your twelve-year?"

"It's basically the same whiskey," he said, "but we—my son, Preston, and I and the staff at Buffalo Trace—taste barrels. We taste every barrel before we bottle. It's vetted a little more seriously because we have a certain flavor profile that we're looking for."

"Do you ever get tired of talking about this?" he was asked.

"I don't talk about anything else," he said.

- 18 -

IT WAS A STRANGE NIGHT. A marketing guy gave a welcome speech about Blade and Bow in which he described this distillery as a "cathedral of bourbon," the kind of talk that makes Julian roll his eyes. He is part of an enormous industry fueled by hype and myth and is both a beneficiary and a critic of that culture. It struck me as strange that the speech didn't mention that the grandson of the man who made it a cathedral was sitting out there in the crowd. Julian never said a disparaging word, and Lord knows I tried. Alas, he's far too savvy and Southern to be visibly upset in public, especially when I have an open notebook, but I could tell this rubbed him the wrong way and left him unsure of how to process it all. He literally had front-row seats as a myth was being created in real time, using his family's story as the buttressing stones of that myth. The Blade and Bow logo even had his grandfather's five keys on it. We sat at a long farm table lit with candles. I wore a fedora with my

Churchill Downs press badge on it, which felt right on the line between appropriate and affected. The food was dressed-down fancy—chef-tuned mashed potatoes and gravy served in Styrofoam KFC cups—and Julian sat down near the end, next to me, listening to people talk with unearned authority about this place that feels as much a part of his family as his own blood.

All this became a little much for him. In the hours after dinner, as the Steep Canyon Rangers played its set, Julian and I went looking for the bathroom, which meant walking the grounds of his family's old distillery and heading to the office. We stepped out of the tent into the darkness. The night echoed with acorns landing on the metal roofs of the rickhouses. Julian stopped suddenly on the walkway leading up to the brick office and white columns, which were lit for maximum drama. I watched him closely. He checked out the trees and the warehouses and the footpaths. There were a dozen memories attached to everything he saw. The darkness and the shadows of the party lights made things come in and out of view, a strange strobing effect that added to the feeling that we'd entered another dimension.

"Oh boy," he said softly.

He pulled out his phone to take a picture. To his left was the screen with the Blade and Bow logo, along with a bright studio light, where guests had been having their pictures taken earlier with a horse. To the right was the open field where Julian used to shoot doves and skeet and hear the shotgun blasts echoing off the corrugated-tin warehouse walls. He waited for the front door to be closed so he could take a picture and then we went inside. Some of the rooms had been changed. Some looked exactly the same, with the wood trim and wainscoting. If he closed his eyes he could still hear Mary Patrick tapping away on her typewriter, and hear his father's voice on the phone, checking in with his sales reps around the country. The old man barked like the World War II tank commander he was until the day he died. Julian and his dad had a complicated relationship; men of different generations with different ways of showing love. Those feelings added layers to his memories as he went inside the miniature Monticello his grandfather had built.

He walked through the offices, peeked into the room where Pappy had moved when his dad took over. Mrs. Nell ran the switchboard over there. Julian stepped inside what was now Tommy Bulleit's office. "I've got pictures of Pappy, my dad, and me standing there with a shotgun in front of the fireplace," he said. "That's the old bathroom; the executive bathroom with the shower. I would come in here after working in the warehouse and take a shower in there."

Soon it felt like it was time to go. This was someone else's space now. He didn't belong. Julian fell quiet. When we got outside, he asked if I would take his picture in front of this building where so many of his photographs of his dad and granddad were taken. The band was loud, the sound pouring out of the tent into the trees.

I snapped the picture and he took my phone to look at himself.

"The cover of the fucking book," Julian said.

He asked me what the title of this thing was gonna be.

"*Cathedral of Bourbon*," I said, and we both laughed in the darkness.

- 19 -

THE PARTY KEPT ROLLING. I found a seat on the couch and caught up with Chenault and Ed, who looked up at the stage with a smile as Julian grabbed a cowbell and sat in with the band. His daughter pretended to be mortified but was secretly proud. What her dad did, rising out of the ashes of the family line that ended at this distillery in 1972, was both a business lesson and a human one. Julian's success felt like a road map, a guide for men to sort out what a son owes his father and what he should feel free to leave in the past. He took the life he'd been born into and rebuilt it so his children might enjoy it, too. Those were the things that hit me as the Derby party downshifted to the last gasps. I needed to leave soon to get some sleep before an early morning racetrack television appearance on ESPN, and Julian would take this party far into the night.

The Steep Canyon Rangers ended its show and someone played

music through the PA while the band packed up its gear. Prince came on. Julian stood around with the band and his daughter while we all sang along to "Purple Rain." The guitar tone felt perfect, the fuzz of the riff and the heavy bass string hit, anchoring the chords in the earth, like the limestone wells beneath our feet. The sound seemed to embody Julian's melancholy and joy, coming back to this place. Instead of letting his family's legacy die in these old buildings, he resurrected it. He is carrying on the work. He's making the trip.

- 20 -

THREE DAYS LATER, Sonia and I went to her doctor for her first
blood test to see if the procedure had worked. It did. She was pregnant. It was a Tuesday, Sonia's friend Cara's birthday. We took that
as a sign. The nurses gave us a tentative test and told us to come
back on Thursday. We made the drive once again. It was Sonia's
brother's birthday. We took that as a sign, too. The blood test came
in positive again, and that confirmed for us that she was pregnant.
The next day I drove to Alabama to visit my boss and dear friend
John Skipper, who was giving the commencement address at the
Tuskegee Institute. John and I shared a mutual love of literature
and a hope that the better angels of the South might one day pre-
vail. That night as we sat in the old plantation home that was now
the university president's house, and as we felt the immense weight
of that change, not only in the faces and stories of my fellow diners
but also in the air, I felt a profound and new sense of rebirth and

of hope as I tried to wish the world I wanted for my child into existence. The positive news sank in slowly. I cried tears of hope and fear, then told the news to my mother, my brother, and my uncle Will—who since the death of my father has become the most important male role model in my life, a real surrogate for me. Will has never had a taste of Pappy Van Winkle, so I made a mental note to get a bottle from Julian to give to him. His smile when I hand it over will remind me of that night in New Orleans outside the Superdome, and of my father, who was present that evening and whenever Uncle Will and I are together.

PART II

- 1 -

THE NIGHT BEFORE THANKSGIVING, I booked tables for thirty at Ramon's, an Italian roadhouse I love in my hometown of Clarksdale, Mississippi. The Ely family always makes me feel welcome, like I've come for dinner at their home. I love the Miller Lite sign glowing in the window and the way people bring their own wine and booze in cases from a bygone era. Some of the older customers bring their own miniature mobile bars, made of leather and embossed with initials. It's my favorite place to eat in the world and I looked forward to sharing it with my family. The Thompsons do Thanksgiving big, a tradition started by my dad and his brothers when their mother died to protect them against the buffeting forces of time and distance, which create the vacuum in which family decay sets in. I've always admired their foresight. Now there are only two brothers left, Will and Michael, and this tradition is being passed to my generation. I worry sometimes that we aren't up to the task. Families stay together because of active decisions, because of patterns that turn into rituals, and they are torn apart most often not by anger or feuds but by careless inertia. Few people in my generation even have a house big enough for sixty Thompsons and friends, wherein we unleash a spread that includes five beef tenderloins, a dozen desserts, two turkeys, a range of wild game and dove stew, and oysters my cousin Charles brought up from the Gulf. We still wear ties to lunch before changing into the proper attire to play a football game and then watch one.

So this year, I added the Wednesday night dinner at Ramon's. I took a bottle of Van Winkle Family Reserve Rye, a gift from Julian, and I went around the room pouring glasses. People understood that opening this bottle was a sign of my appreciation, the myth of Pappy serving as a show of respect and love. Each glass honored this tradition and offered the wish that it might continue. My father is buried just up the road from Ramon's. After everyone finished, my brother and I left the restaurant together to visit him. I carried the empty bottle with me to the car. We drove into the darkness in silence. I pulled into the cemetery and placed the bottle on my father's grave. Neither my brother nor I spoke. He just looked at me and nodded.

~ 2 ~

JULIAN AND I SETTLED INTO A PATTERN. When our schedules aligned, I'd meet him somewhere: Kentucky, Michigan, San Francisco. When I arrived he'd make jokes about how these trips would never, ever result in a book. I loved spending time with him and Sissy because what Julian lacked in the instinct to reflect, he made up for as a host. He'd allude to "difficulties" and "stress" when describing what happened in his father's life—and then in his own life—after the family lost the Stitzel-Weller distillery. He rarely went much further. I'm not saying he avoids stuff, at least not consciously, but he is happier now than he was living his old life, when he spent two decades scratching together enough money to source whiskey and then run it through the bottling plant he owned near Lawrenceburg, Kentucky, which is closer to Lexington than Louisville, west of the Four Roses and Woodford Reserve distilleries. Whiskey aficionados love the bourbon he bottled there because he used his once-in-a-generation palate to taste different barrels of various ages and provenance and knew which ones he should blend to make great bourbon. He worked with one hand tied behind his back financially, and the work he did there remains the stuff of legend, because his skills allowed him to put out fine bourbon where other men would have failed. That's how he built a reputation separate from his famous last name.

I told him I wanted him to take me to Lawrenceburg. That's where the real soul of Pappy Van Winkle's Family Reserve lived. If the story outsiders tell about Julian has to do with cult bourbons and stingy allocations, the story his family tells about him is about the years he spent in Lawrenceburg.

I also just wanted to see the place where one day it rained vodka. It's one of his favorite stories. At some point during his Lawrenceburg tenure, he'd taken a contract bottling vodka for a guy who ended up not paying him. Julian desperately needed the money and would take any flyer who walked through the door. A truck would pull up outside and empty the pure grain alcohol into a large holding tank, which was then released a little at a time into a seven hundred–gallon reservoir connected to the bottling line. The bottling plant was three or four stories tall. That is about to become important.

A guy working down on the line screamed, "Fuck!" People dove to find cover and yelled in fear. Julian came running. He found the entire tower raining 190-proof grain neutral spirits. He'd forgotten to turn off the pump, and so when the holding tank filled up, the liquor had nowhere else to go. Booze was just pouring through every crack in the floor, rolling in a waterfall down the stairs. Julian sprinted to the pump and turned it off and came back inside to find his employees soaked like wet dogs. That was when he noticed the entire place smelled like a lumber mill. He won't ever forget that. It really smelled exactly like freshly sawed two-by-fours. The 190-proof firewater stripped away a century of grime and muck and gunk off all the boards and now everything looked brand-new, like it had all just been built.

"It was raining all the way down," he said. "Put that in the book."

- 3 -

ON A TYPICALLY WARM KENTUCKY MORNING, Julian headed over from his house to the Buffalo Trace distillery. I parked in the lot down below the rickhouses and headed into the gift shop, where I found him signing decanters for a man who had brought his three grandsons with him. The man's son was getting into the bourbon business up the road, he said—Three Boys Farm Distillery, it's called—and he was clearly in awe of Julian, who posed for pictures. When the man started espousing his political theories, Julian disengaged and we walked back through the museum and gift shop, where the ladies who manage the place keep a running stack of stuff left by people for Julian to sign. His kids think it's hilarious that anyone might want his autograph; this late-in-life third act still seems like some elaborate prank pulled on all of them, and eventually the ruse will be revealed.

It smelled like whiskey outside, at least to me. Julian always jokes that it smells like money. Buffalo Trace has been his home since he made the deal to escape the collapsing bottling line we were going to see. The distillery sits in a little valley, and the road winds down into a canyon of brick smokestacks and hulking rickhouses full of barrels. There's a café in nearby Frankfort where he likes to go—the owner makes good moonshine, he tells me—so we headed into town. That's where the state government is located, which always prompts him to go on a roll about taxes. It had been a few months since the Kentucky Derby and I still wasn't entirely clear on how the family went from owning a beautiful, sprawling distillery on the outskirts of Louisville to Julian fighting to survive in a back-road bottling plant. Julian explained the vote again, how his dad's sister sided with the minority shareholders to force the sale. But he also told me something new. "We couldn't have hung on to it," he said. "There's no way. The whiskey business wasn't good, way before its time, so to speak."

There were several interconnected reasons why the bourbon market cratered in the 1960s. First of all, the vodka lobby finally changed the laws to give itself a designation. Before, vodka had been called "neutral grain spirit," which sounded like something the town drunk keeps in a flask before pissing himself on a bench. Vodka, however, sounded like something James Bond drank. In fact he did, and bourbon historians actually point to the Bond effect. The industry panicked to the initial wavering of the market, which made it all worse: raising the barrel entry proof to make more product, which forever reduced the quality of the whiskey, and then making light bourbon that went better in cocktail mixes, or so the advertising department thought. But most of all, the historians say that the same conflict playing out between Julian and his father was actually driving the collapse of bourbon. This was a time of rebellion. Bourbon was what your father drank. Nobody wanted to be like their fathers. People looked for new things to drink in this new age. This is the market Julian Proctor Van Winkle Jr. inherited from his father, Pappy. The old tank commander didn't understand why the world had suddenly changed on him.

- 4 -

SONIA DIDN'T WANT TO TELL PEOPLE she was pregnant. She didn't want the attention or the sympathy if something went wrong again. I worried about that, of course, and about everything else. I worried about what this child would need from me. I set up a college fund. My own parents served as such a great example. Both loved me unconditionally and showed that love every day, as well as an unshakable belief in me and my dreams, no matter how unlikely they seemed. That's what I wanted to provide, more than anything else: a safe harbor of encouragement.

I wanted her to have my dad's sense of wonder and fairness. He always celebrated other people's success and believed that greatness wasn't a zero-sum game. You were only ever competing against yourself and your own limitations. Someone else's joy was never your sadness, he always taught us. I wanted her to have my mother's sense of unconditional love and her toughness. Nobody is better in a crisis than my mom; she possesses a fire and love and strength that words alone can't describe. I wanted our daughter to carry the best of them, and of me and us, while leaving the worst behind. I wished I could swallow all our faults so that those things could die with me and leave her unencumbered. The scary part, I realized, was that she would learn little from anything I said and more from the things I did, the things she'd be intently watching me do.

Talking to Julian's kids helped me start to keep notes about the kind of father I wanted to be. They tell funny stories about going back and watching the thousands of home videos he took of them. Once the triplets had a funeral for their baby dolls and, as they wail about burying dead babies, you can hear Julian on the camera's microphone trying and failing not to laugh. "When we were kids, his love language was spending time with us," his daughter Chenault said. "He is a family man and was always around. He is easygoing and doesn't do well with confrontation and was not the disciplinarian. That naturally fell on Mom, which I know got old for her to have to be the bad guy all the time. When she had had enough he would be the enforcer of whatever needed enforcing at her request, and I could tell she had put him up to it and I just couldn't take it seriously. I remember holding back laughing when he was disciplining me for something, knowing it had come straight from Mom."

– 5 –

JULIAN SHAPED HIMSELF into a different kind of father than the one he had growing up. He was more patient, involved, easy, but he also deeply admired his dad, and how he lived, worked, and shouldered the burden of Pappy's shadow. Julian's dad worked hard; a bull of a man. Once when the distillery workers went on strike, he rode through the picket lines on the running boards of a truck, carrying his shotgun. Nobody dared fuck with him. Alas, that spirit couldn't make people want to drink bourbon. Finally, unable to fend off his relatives, he made the decision that he'd rather stop fighting than alienate his family. He faced an impossible choice. Would he destroy the family in order to defend it? For the only time in his life, the tank captain surrendered. He regretted it for the rest of his life.

"We didn't get cash," Julian explained to me. "We got Norton Simon stock. You ever heard of that company? They were a conglomerate. They owned Tanqueray, Johnnie Walker, Canada Dry,

I guess the soft drinks. *McCall's* magazine, Avis, all kinds of different shit, and they wanted a distillery so they ended up with it. So we got Norton Simon stock and it went down to like two dollars a share one year and we're all going, 'Oh my God, what the fuck is about to happen now?' and that probably helped my father get prostate cancer I'm sure. But then it bounced back and everyone ended up selling it, getting rid of it, which was okay, it finally worked out."

When Julian's dad moved out of his office—Tommy Bulleit's office now—he wanted to work but didn't have a place to go. He wasn't the kind to go find a beach. So he got an office in a building on Brownsboro Road in Louisville, a block or so from Patrick's Bar, one of the world's great dives, and he hired a secretary and started to buy whiskey from his old distillery and others to bottle a private label. He called it Old Rip Van Winkle. Julian remains in that office today and now his son, Preston, is in there, too. For nine years, Julian's dad bought whiskey from Stitzel-Weller, which then bottled it for him as a favor and a sign of respect for the family. In 1981, he died after his short fight against prostate cancer. He rarely if ever talked about the great shame of losing Stitzel-Weller. The pain was worse to him than getting shot during the war.

"It killed him," his daughter Sally flatly told me one night at dinner. The stress and the cancer were merely complications from the mortal wound of losing the most important part of himself.

- 6 -

JULIAN AND HIS DAD were men of different times. That's how it is with fathers and sons. The act of spanning a generational divide is the single most important thing either person will do in their lifetime; the relationship depends on making that leap successfully.

With my own father, I remember so clearly a moment in 1986, when he called me into the master bedroom where the final round of the Masters played on the television. It was the day before his fortieth birthday, I realized years later. I didn't know then what that meant, but I do now—how a man is forced to examine his life and make an accounting of everything he wanted to be and everything he has actually become, to sort out dreams from failures, and to realize for the first time that the road he is on is the only road he'll ever travel. At forty, reinvention is pretty much dead. You are the man you were always going to be. Except . . . "Jack Nicklaus is going to win the Masters, son, and you've got to watch this," he told me. "You will remember this for the rest of your life."

Together we watched a forty-six-year-old man find a lost piece of his younger self. My father cried that afternoon. I don't remember ever seeing him cry before.

For the first few years after his death, my defining memory of my father's passing was of landing at the Memphis airport. My family hadn't told me the news so I thought I was flying home to sit vigil. On the escalator down into baggage claim, I saw my mother step out from behind a pillar. My brother stood next to her. The escalator seemed to slow down as he just shook his head. When I got to the bottom, my mother said, "Your sweet daddy died."

My father dreamed of attending the Masters. When I started working as a sportswriter, I'd go every year, and I promised to take him. I never did. That regret ate away at me, and so I dealt with it the only way I knew how: I wrote a story. Called "Holy Ground," it was about our relationship with that golf tournament and how it was a proxy for something much larger. It was written when the wound of Daddy's passing was still fresh, and so it soothed me, but I also hoped that it might keep some of his spirit alive. I've gotten hundreds of messages about it. I've had strangers at the airport stop me to tell me what it meant to them and their father. I love it when people talk to me about this story, because that means it has done its work. My mother wrote me a few years ago and said, *"Just reread holy ground. always do this time of year. It continues to be a gift beyond measure. ilu! xooxoxoxox mama."*

~ 7 ~

MOST EVERY MAN COMPETES WITH HIS FATHER and imitates his father, lives in fear of disappointing, and craves approval, and on the extreme ends of this potentially fraught relationship, a man often spends his entire adult life trying to be exactly like his father or nothing like him. I loved the book Julian's sister Sally wrote, for its comprehensive history, sure, but mostly because I got to see their father through her eyes. The lens of a daughter and the lens of a son will never be the same. It's helpful to get to know the man she knew before seeing the man his son worked alongside.

I enjoyed spending time with Sally. She's smart, beautiful, and passionate about preserving the history of Kentucky. She wrote another book called *Saving Kentucky*, and she devotes a lot of energy to helping me remember their past. That passion started with her book about the distillery. Seeing her family's second home under the control and care of others leaves her in distress. A friend of mine went with her on a tour once, and as she walked the grounds, she wept so noticeably that he asked if she was okay. It's all still raw for the Van Winkles. Her book, *But Always Fine Bourbon*, in a lot of ways, was about reclaiming her own memories. She wanted a record for others, yes, but also for herself, as proof that any of it happened. Her father comes alive on the page. She describes his athletic build and his "gorgeous" legs and his bald head and olive skin. You can hear him laugh when she describes it. An Ivy League man, he wanted his salesmen to be up on all the current events and gave them free subscriptions to all the magazines in which Old Fitz advertised. As I read, I could only hope that one day I'd have a daughter who looked at me with the admiration Sally felt for the man the Stitzel-Weller staff called Mr. Julian. At bedtime, reading stories aloud, he could do all the voices. He could be found in cashmere jackets or hunting pants "full of bird blood and holes," she wrote, and no matter how hard he tried, he couldn't be quiet. Their mother often said, "Shhhhhh, Van!"

They never knew how bad the whiskey business had gotten. Mr. Julian never complained, an army officer to his core. He stayed at the office late. His plate almost always waited for him in the warmer. He never complained. One of his favorite sayings about hard times was, "Blossom, bring on the beans."

He and his only son could not have been more different.

"Night and day," his sister Sally said, laughing. "Dad was really gregarious and a bull in a china shop and just out there."

I'd heard a lot of stories about Mr. Julian, read a lot about him, too, and it seemed pretty clear that Sally made a conscious decision in her book to write about the best side of a complicated man. I understood completely. I've written about my father a lot, too, and while I am not ashamed of his flaws, I did think it was my right to focus on the parts that rang most true to me. It was my job as a firstborn son to protect him in death as I had been unable to do in life.

- 8 -

MY FATHER DRANK—A LOT.

I've never written that before in all the thousands of words I've written about him, although I've hinted at it. But I've concluded not mentioning it makes no sense, since the omertà that is so important in my family also strips from him the courage it took to find his hard-won freedom. His dad, Frazier, my grandfather, drank a lot, too. A brilliant man forced to drop out of college to run the family farm after his own dad died, he never got over the gulf between the life he wanted and the life he ended up living. I'm wondering right now, for the first time, how much my dad internalized those fears and the demons that quieted them. Big Frazier liked Canadian Club and lived in shame at his inability to stop drinking it. He begged his boys to be stronger than him. My dad made good on his father's unrealized dreams of sobriety. He admitted he had a problem, he attended meetings and did his most vital work, in terms of both helping people and big paydays. And while I won't bare any more of his soul here, because he's not alive to give his blessing, I do think my dad had real greatness in him that he never fully tapped.

When I thought about the child who would join our family, I was often overcome with grief that she would never get to meet the amazing and totally original man who was my father. He was magnetic and kind and generous and taught me so many lessons, like to never feel jealous of other people's success, and to try to see the best in people and to have empathy for whatever might be causing or fueling their worst behaviors. There wasn't a strange roadside diner specializing in stewed rabbit that he ever passed without stopping. He played air drums to Motown classics when he drove. I cannot count the number of times we listened to the soundtrack from *The Big Chill*. He loved to go to the beach and buy a cooler of seafood and spend his vacation in the kitchen, cooking up big dinners that we would all share. The sound of the ocean makes me picture his smile. I've got a photo of him as a young man in my office, and I'm looking at it right now, and it's crazy how the smile he's wearing in that photo is the same one I knew so well as his son. He was a lifelong Democrat mainly because he thought Republicans were "mean," and he was able to go into the most country, good-old-boy places and raise money for people like Michael Dukakis. He wore seersucker with style. He loved old war movies. He loved bologna and hoop cheese sandwiches from old country stores. He loved my mother deeply and unconditionally. In the years after he died, she would find flashlight after flashlight stashed around the house. He'd gone and bought dozens of them and hidden them, where they might be discovered one by one, as a reminder that he would always be there, shining. That story sums him up best to me. He thought of the grand gesture and then did it.

When my dad's cancer got him at age fifty-eight, he ran out of time. He needed more time. I'm biased but I believe with his brain and charisma he could have been governor of Mississippi. He brought that kind of energy with him into a room. I cannot remember what his voice sounded like, but I will never forget how the atmosphere in a room changed when that voice entered it. His unfulfilled potential has been my greatest fear and motivator. For the past two decades, I've worked like a maniac at the expense of so many other things in my life, trying on some level to be successful enough for the both of us. That was my mission and along with it came my greatest fear: What if I self-destructed on the road to success? Might I be so focused on redeeming my father that I wouldn't slow down enough to really understand the warnings of his life, that I'd build something great and then, chased by the same old demons, watch it crumble—or, even worse, tear it down myself? Meeting Julian and making him talk about his family made me ask myself the same question I'd been asking him: What did I owe my late father? What did I owe a grandfather I never met? What is demanded of a son or a daughter? What was demanded of me?

- 9 -

JULIAN OFTEN DESCRIBES HIS OWN FATHER with the same simple phrase: he was a tank captain in World War II. We all develop one-line descriptions that use one biographical detail to say everything. Julian didn't say his father was a legend in the whiskey business, although he was. He doesn't say he was distant from his name-sake son but doting with his grandchildren. No, his description goes back to his dad's time in the Pacific. He was a tank com-mander. He rolled over anything in his way. Julian sometimes felt rolled over. The outsized nature of his father's strength and heroism kept Julian from seeing that he himself was more like Pappy than his old man was, and that he didn't need to be anything other than himself.

Our fathers are often mysteries to us and therefore we are often mysteries to ourselves. Self-awareness only comes with time if it comes at all. Julian was so busy dealing with the man he wasn't that he didn't really spend time to get to know the man he was. My dad didn't roll over me, but he did cast a big enough shadow that I knew I'd have to eclipse or else grow stagnant in the shade. I wanted to be able to stand confidently next to the idea of him. Julian also contended with the expansive idea of his father, a man who would rather die than let his men go into battle without him, not because he wanted medals but because they counted on him. He was not an easy man. Every morning he did his old military exercises: bicycles, jumping jacks, and sit-ups. When he needed to silence his mind, he'd get a buddy and go and chop down trees, hollering war cries the whole time.

Even in photos he's intimidating. A six-foot-four former football player at Princeton, Captain Julian P. Van Winkle Jr. led Company A of the Forty-fourth Tank Battalion from island to island through the Pacific. When he had a day free from combat, hunkered in tents and in muddy holes during the fierce rainy season, he read the account reports from Stitzel-Weller his dad sent him. He was thirty years old, ancient to his men. Julian Jr. landed with his unit on the island of Leyte in 1944, near the tip of the spear of Douglas MacArthur's return to the Philippines. The best account of their terrible, bloody slog comes from the book *Bourbon & Bullets*, a collection of stories about whiskey men who went to war. The book brings the battle alive: Van Winkle's company helped lead a frontal assault at a place known as Breakneck Ridge. His personal tank was named Old Fitz, after his most famous bourbon. They fought through a monsoon. By week three, the pace of the advance had slowed.

Julian's dad got out of his tank to direct his men, ignoring wither-ing enemy fire. A sniper shot him, the bullet going through his right hand and his stomach, exiting out his back.

"Damn, that stings!" a soldier heard him yell.

He turned down an offer to go home, and fought with doctors in the Dutch New Guinea hospital to be allowed back to his unit. Stuck in bed recovering, he raged against the injustice of it all. Survivor's guilt ate at him. Nine days after he left the unit, his re-placement was killed. As he waited for the hospital administrators to decide, he wrote to Pappy, "I have died a thousand deaths for fear I'll go to the States. I will go to any length to stay here."

He won this battle and rejoined Company A in time to take Manila. There he saw the liberated prisoners of the Bataan Death March and reflected on the brutality and cost of such a war. He wrote to Pappy: "Perhaps it is almost justice, dad, that we should have to go through war every so often to pay for the peace years— so filled with plenty and pleasure as compared with the other peo-ple on earth."

Sitting at lunch with me in Frankfort before driving out to the old bottling line in Lawrenceburg, Julian described the letters, which revolved around his dad's two favorite topics for discussion: the Stitzel-Weller distillery and eliminating the enemy. "He's talk-ing to Pappy about the business," Julian told me, "because he went to work for Pappy and then he went to the war and then got shot and was really pissed he couldn't continue killing the Japanese. He talks about that a whole lot for about two months in the hospital.

He finally got back out there and got a Purple Heart and a Silver Star and he was a badass."

During his recent cancer treatment, Julian and his sisters pored over these letters. His dad's handwriting was terrible; Pappy didn't like that his boy was left-handed and made him switch, which Julian's dad always blamed for his chicken scratch. The man in the letters sometimes felt like a stranger to his son.

"Some of them were pretty intimate," he said.

"Did he ever tell war stories?" I asked.

"I never really asked him," Julian said. "Probably scared to, probably wasn't ever close enough to him to sit down and ask him. I know I really cared, but it just never came up to me because he was always going to be around. And all of a sudden he was gone. I wish I'd asked him about what it was really like, and how many people did you kill and what was it like. It had to be just really ugly. I just never did that, unfortunately."

- 10 -

BEING WITH JULIAN MADE ME THINK about craft in America. About how our work ethic combines with the secular myths of bootstrap success to make people predisposed to respect craftsmanship. Something to occupy our hyper-American ambition and our desire to make something—to find God in our labor and in the fruits of it. Spending so much time talking to him about his family's craft made me consider my own.

I lived my early life on a blissfully unaware autopilot until one night in high school, when I read a book called *North Toward Home* by the native Mississippian and legendary *Harper's* magazine editor Willie Morris. In the book, he talked about how magazines and journalism and the desire to tell hard truths about new places— and about familiar places we knew too well—gave him his life, and his purpose—his avenue of escape. When I started that book, I figured I'd go to law school and come home and take over my dad's small-town firm. When I finished, I had a goal and a purpose. I'd be a journalist—a career that aligned with my deepest wants and protective urges, both in how it would let me roam and in how it would let me avoid myself by diving into the lives of others. I've always been happiest when dreaming of escape. From my earliest memories, my greatest solace and focus came while in movement, from small actions like pacing while answering flash cards to planning elaborate road trips I knew I'd never take. When I look back at my early life, everything I read and watched and loved and hoped and even feared came from this desire to fly far away.

I had the desire but not the mechanism. Then I read Willie Morris's book. The next morning—I'd read through the night, locked in and aggressively turning pages—I announced to my parents that his words had given me focus. Turned out, they both knew Morris. He grew up in Yazoo City, the closest real town to the tiny farming community where my dad was born and raised. A few days later, a signed copy of *North Toward Home* arrived, with a note from Willie that said how glad he was that this book had struck such a chord with me. Willie is the one who suggested the University of Missouri for journalism school, where I went to college. During spring break of my junior year, in 2000, I went to New York with my best friend, Seth Wickersham, to try to make those dreams into something real. We both wanted to be magazine writers, like Dan Jenkins, like Gary Smith, like Willie Morris. Seth had interviews all over town, at *ESPN The Magazine*, *Sports Illustrated*,

and *The New York Times*. I was more of a tagalong. His meeting at
ESPN Mag went pretty well. Mine did not. The editors at the
magazine forgot about me, so I sat out there for an hour or two, on
a bench by the security guard until someone noticed. There was a
sign above my head that read VISITORS. In front of me, through a
big glass wall, was the world I wanted to enter. The metaphor was
unmistakable.

I survived the magazine editors who had me waiting outside the
ESPN visitors sign. When that office closed, a friend got the sign
and mailed it to me, as a kind of scalp. It's hanging in my house.
Below it, in a box, I keep letters from my dad. He wrote me a lot.
Not long ago, Mama found a file folder in which he'd stored a copy
of every letter he ever sent me. She sent me a photo of one of them,
written after I'd been rejected by nearly every newspaper in America for an internship.

Dear Wright,

Momma told me you did not get the responses you
wanted to hear about summer 2000's internships. Don't
worry or fret too much. The main thing is that one day,
they will have wished they could have gotten to know you
personally—to witness your talents, your drive, your personality. Hang in there. God has been good to you.

Love, Daddy

- 11 -

JULIAN STARTED TO SHARE LETTERS his dad had sent home from
the war, some transcribed by him and his sisters, Sally and Kitty,
and others just scanned and emailed.

October 17, 1944

Dear Dad,

I have a very tall stack of mail from you and I am
ashamed not to have answered before now. Never have I
found it so difficult to write letters yet the last day or two
I have ground out many a one. Since we can't take any
letters or envelopes addressed to us as they might inform
the enemy of our organization, I am answering every last
one before we get off. Unfortunately I shall have to answer

all of yours in one letter. Everything else seems rather trivial as compared with the job at hand and that's the reason I don't seem to be able to think of much to say. This is real adventure Dad, an A-1 high-class fiction material and I only wish I could tell you all the things I know about the projected plan. It is fascinating of course and an undertaking of the greatest magnitude has undoubtedly been in the works for months although I understand the schedule has been stepped up considerably.

We are all totally sure that it will be another MacArthur success. Mainly hitting the Jap where he ain't. The guys in GHQ are mighty clever at this game. There's no army on earth that could stop the force of this attack. I have been tremendously interested in all the info you all have given me about the plant—the new well, the cooling tower, the holiday whiskey and prices etc.

I received the nicest letter from Mr. Willett. I certainly did enjoy it. Please thank him for me.

I haven't heard anything more from Bud. I was awfully glad to hear of the outcome of Grigg's-Cooper deal. I admire your brass to have put it to them like you did. Apparently you all feel not the slightest concern over the obtaining of plenty customers postwar. I was immensely interested in the Omaha news clipping showing the corn outlooks. Lord, with a 3 billion bushel crop, they should let us make bourbon from now on.

I read with great pleasure Dad your letter about giving us the bonds. I can only say thanks again to you for that as well as for the many other wonderful things you have done for me all my life. I hope I justify the faith and trust you have placed in me. Best of all was the money you gave mother. I know that made her very happy. I hope this finds all of you well and happy, Dad. Don't let my gals worry and have faith in yourself. I'll be writing you in a week or 10 days. Again thank you and mother for making Katie and Sally's lives so happy while I'm on [this] little "business" trip.

Affectionately always,
Brud

The letters paint a portrait of a man far from home. Often he'd ask about Julian's mother, Katie, and about the world that was continuing even as he was engaged in a cosmic struggle a half planet away. He liked hearing about what laws were being passed that concerned their business and how the relationship with the all-important cooperage was going. You can see a man traveling in his mind back down Limestone Lane, past the stone posts at the entrance, walking in the cool shade of the rickhouses or carrying a shotgun in the crook of his arm, scanning the sky for birds. Writing letters seemed to take him back home even more than receiving them. He just wanted to be part of his old life. In one letter from

1945 he wrote: *The company party sounded like lots of fun. I know everyone had lots of fun. Wish I could have been there—especially for the ball game and to get a cold glass of beer. The beer we get has been all right but there is never enough ice to cool it, I just can't go for hot beer.*

– 12 –

ONE AFTERNOON, sitting with Sissy Van Winkle, I asked what Julian's dad was like.

"Overbearing, powerful, strong, sort of tender," she said. "Tender to me, tender to the children, but not tender to Julian. Busy, busy, busy always socially busy, working. Adored Katie Van Winkle, his wife, but did not know how to slow down to give her the attention that she wanted."

He never stopped writing letters. In 1977, he learned that his son, Julian, had quit his job as a salesman at a Louisville clothing store named Rodes-Rapier. He asked Sissy if Julian might consider working for him. It was like junior high school a bit, check yes or no, a window into how much of their love for one another often got lost in translation.

"Ask him," she said finally.

So on May 31, his dad dictated a letter to his secretary, Lois

Devlin. Julian doesn't remember ever getting the letter. He found the notes years later.

Dear Jule,

I have always hoped that someday we would be in business together. You have impressed me with your persistence in your job—your ability to make friends and your total personality which is mild and pleasant and agreeable. I am also pleased with your attitude as a husband and your success in marriage—and in your judgment to pick a first-class woman for a wife and in your tendency to be thrifty and a good man around the house.

You have apparently decided that you don't want to make a career of working for somebody else. I like this independent attitude although I would rather you had observed some other companies—or jobs or industries more closely.

Every father wants his son to do well and I had the chance to work for my dad. His industrious attitude and his other qualities fascinated me—and he had a going business.

We don't have that much here. They consist of two parts; first the ceramics and their collectors. Number two, the tiny business just started and not doing very well on old Rip Van Winkle. 1843 is another possibility if we could set it up properly with Mac and Chenault and if OFD would bottle it for us. There is some future there if it were worked properly and if we were lucky.

But this would give you a chance to learn how business is conducted. Learn office routine—learn details from Lois and see if it appealed and if there was a real future.

You have some habits that are not bad but I don't admire and I would feel free to admonish you about those if I felt they were mitigating your effectiveness. I have always done the same with anyone who worked for me and have not been the worse off for it. I am not sure if you'd find enough to do here but if you are ambitious to build the business and if I only give some direction but never have to tell you the importance of work and learning the business, then there is a possibility of developing this into a business really worthwhile.

You will have to make the effort but if you are enterprising and off and running—a go-getter—then there won't be enough hours in the day to read, and accomplish all there is. There never has been for me.

Julian's dad has been dead now for thirty-eight years. We went one day to visit his grave, in the same Louisville cemetery as Colonel Sanders and Muhammad Ali, buried right next to Pappy. That's where the two men would want to be, side by side, like they were for much of their lives. Julian is old now. He's got the same white hair and bald head as Pappy. He's got his grandfather's gift for selling a story—for living that story, without pretense or affectation, so that the promise each bottle holds is a piece of his authentic self and therefore yours. It's a real magic trick. But he's also the tank commander, too, which is what kept him afloat in those decades after his father died but before the bourbon industry boomed. If he is channeling the spirit of Pappy in this third act, then it was the spirit of his father he took with him on those daily drives to his dilapidated bottling line. Julian lived both their lives to finally fully inhabit his own.

- 13 -

WE'D BEEN TALKING A LOT about Lawrenceburg. Julian told me
stories about the low beams on which he often cracked his skull,
and the rats and the flooding, and how the bottling line broke all
the time. Our plan was to leave lunch and drive twenty-two miles
south, away from the soft rolling green of wealthy horse country,
closer to the winding mountain hollers of moonshine country. Bourbon lives on the edge of both worlds. It's easy to forget the renegade
past in the shiny Buffalo Trace distillery but much harder out where
Julian bottled all those years. He painted a picture of a building that
looked less like a place to make fine bourbon and more like a place
where you'd successfully hide a body.

Our plan for the day was clear, and yet when we got into the
car, Julian started driving toward Louisville, not his old bottling
plant. I didn't notice because I didn't really have a fucking clue

where I was. We listened to Howard Stern—whom he loves—and talked about our families and Preston's coming divorce, and about our mutual love of fast German cars. Then it hit him.

"Oh shit!" he said. "I forgot to go to Lawrenceburg."

"We'll go tomorrow," I said.

- 14 -

THERE ARE A FEW COOL HOTELS IN LOUISVILLE, so I always have a good place to set up shop. There's the Brown Hotel and the Galt House. My old favorite, a dive motel out near Churchill Downs called the Executive Inn West—with the weirdest, wildest hotel bar in America, where rodeo cowboys swung one night from the chandeliers—has been torn down and replaced with something normal, square, and boring. On this particular trip, I stayed at a combo hotel–art gallery in a bizarre ground-floor suite. The plan was to meet Julian and his son-in-law, Ed, at the bar there and then have dinner.

I love being with Julian or his son, Preston, in a bar that fetishizes bourbon. Sadly, I wasn't there for the best bourbon-fetish bar moment. Once, in New York, Preston leaned against a bar and ordered a Van Winkle how he drinks it, as Julian drinks it, as Julian Jr. and Pappy drank it: on the rocks with a twist. The bartender snootily told him he didn't feel right serving such fine bourbon like that. Preston grinned. He paused, for dramatic effect, and then delivered the kill shot: *Well, sir, that sure is disappointing, given that's how my grandfather and father taught me to drink it, and my family made the stuff after all. Hi, I'm Preston Van Winkle.* . . . When I heard that story, I laughed at a hipster getting a lesson that bourbon is supposed to be a vehicle and not a destination. When a bourbon-nerd friend heard it, though, he got angry at Preston for disrespecting someone's passion, which I do not understand at all but trust him enough to take seriously.

When Julian and Ed arrived at the hotel bar and we all got settled and watered—Julian drinks wheated bourbon, as you might imagine, and if the place doesn't have one of about six or seven brands, he'll go with a vodka tonic. I started asking him more about the Lawrenceburg plant. After his dad died, he'd floated around to bottlers to get his whiskey on the shelves but realized he needed his own base of operations. He went far from the lush distillery grounds of his youth.

Those were hard years for him.

"What was difficult about it?" I asked.

"Well, let's see . . . old building . . . This was '83 when I bought it and I sold it in 2002 for the same thing I bought it for. There was a bottling house and a cased-goods place and three barrel warehouses, one of which was usable. But the place had been there forever and shit was just breaking down, the creek flooded, fucking decanters floating around in the basement. Roof leaking, equipment not working. Bumping my head on the warehouse. Raccoons would go in the warehouse and shit in the elevator. Raccoons are the nastiest animals on earth, by the way, they're just gross and there was just raccoon shit all over the place."

Here's the thing about all these horror stories. He grew up a sort of prince, sent to the finest Southern boarding school and then to romp his way through college. All the down years are funny now, sitting in a fancy hotel bar that serves the world's most sought-after bourbon that bears his family name. It all feels somehow preordained. That's not how it felt as it was happening. Everything about his whiskey operation in Lawrenceburg, when compared with the beautiful, pristine campus his grandfather and father ran, seemed like part of a cruel, extended metaphor for how far this once-grand family had fallen. *Life* magazine once featured Pappy's genteel Kentucky Derby party in its pages, with pictures of frosted julep cups engraved with J.P.VANW. And now his grandson was wading through a flooded basement, dodging raccoon shit. That's not the life of easy gentility for which Julian had been raised.

"I had an old 1970 Dodge truck that had thirteen thousand miles on it from going from the warehouse to the bottling house, which is like a quarter mile, back and forth for millions of years. . . . I was fixing that fucking truck half the time. I learned how to put in new alternators. You just gotta learn by the seat of your pants. One of my employees put a clutch in there. Thank goodness. I couldn't do that. The starter kept going out and the alternators and shit. I spent almost every day of my life in that son of a bitch."

Listening to him, I sometimes wonder if his ultimate goal wasn't to succeed in Lawrenceburg but to fail with honor. As if the point wasn't to sustain the success of his family but to replicate the work ethic and the dedication—to leave it all on the field, if we're throwing around sports metaphors. Julian would laugh at such a suggestion. He's a guy who gets up and handles that day's business, one foot in front of the other, which is its own kind of zen. He also wouldn't like that I called him zen.

"I'm just glad I got rid of it. And some guy has got it now and I went by there a few months ago and it's really scary looking. I think he's living there. There were some bad things crawling around that place at night. I just can't imagine. But it served its purpose; it created the Pappy Van Winkle brand. That's what we should call the book: *A Weird Thing That Happened: The Pappy Van Winkle Story*."

That's why I want him to take me out to Lawrenceburg.

- 15 -

MANY BOURBON DISTILLERIES sell you a fake story that their corporate overlords try to make sure never gets punctured. Julian is the opposite. His biography gives him as much legitimacy as anyone in town, and yet he is not the crowned king of a dynasty. He saw his family sell its whiskey business and he went away to try to rebuild it, or to keep some small piece of it alive. He did it with the help of countless people, many of whom remembered his grandfather and were called to action by their loyalty and respect. Julian needed a lot of help in Lawrenceburg.

"How hard was it to find people to repair those old bottling machines?" I asked him.

"I actually called Jimmy Russell once a month, the Wild Turkey master distiller," Julian said. "He's the oldest, last one left."

Wild Turkey had long ago left behind whatever archaic systems Julian was still forced to use, being a big, modern bourbon brand like Pappy's Stitzel-Weller used to be. But some of the old code still mattered. Russell had guys on staff who were old enough to re-member tinkering with whatever Julian ran in Lawrenceburg. So he'd send help. Those are the kindnesses that Julian won't ever forget, and if you love Pappy but can't get it, maybe raise a glass of 101 Wild Turkey instead.

"How did he help?" I asked.

"Well, he would send his mechanic over because the filler wasn't working," he said. "One day the thing just quit, and so . . . 'Jimmy, can you send one of your guys over here . . . I got no idea what the hell is going on.' At the bottom of this tank, where I'd captured the whis-key, there's an elbow joint down there that had two clamps on it, one here and one here, so I unclamped the elbow and took it off because I thought something had gotten caught in it. So that came off and nothing's in there, so the guy finally gets his flashlight and looks in the tube going to the filler. One of the little rags we use to clean shit up with—some dumb motherfucker had dropped it in the tank and it sucked it up into the filler . . . clogged it up completely. Pulls this thing out with a coat hanger. . . . 'There's your problem!'"

Julian admires men like Jimmy Russell.

Russell is a famously long-tenured master distiller and ran Wild Turkey at the same time Pappy ran Stitzel-Weller. He's part of the old tribe of bourbon people who compete, sure, but who also help one another out; a connection to the farming culture that gave birth to the spirit. Not long ago, my cousin Thomas raced to get his cotton out of the fields before a coming torrential rainstorm. A neighbor finished his own crop around five p.m., and called up Thomas and asked if he could use the help. Thomas said yes. The man brought his equipment over and worked all night, the last of the cotton picked just before the clouds opened and the storm began. That kind of neighborly instinct is vanishing in a business run by brand managers, accountants, and private equity firms. People call Jimmy "the Buddha of Bourbon." He started at Wild Turkey sweeping floors as a nineteen-year-old: that was 1954. Bourbon was the number one spirit in America. Ike was president. Pappy was seventy-nine. Julian was five. Grantland Rice died that year. The first Fender Stratocaster came off the line. On July 5, Elvis Presley stepped in front of a microphone at Sun Studio on Union Avenue in Memphis for the first time. Julian's father, a war hero and executive at his family's business, looked to a future much like his past. He had no way of knowing that his extinction had already been set in motion, that the cultural forces unleashed by Elvis and those California-made guitars would tear down his world, and that his son would be left with the wreckage and a deeply personal mandate to try to put it all back together again.

- 16 -

WE SAT AROUND A TABLE at the hotel restaurant in Louisville. I'd eaten a lot of meals with Julian by now and had come to enjoy these marathons most of all. Julian is at his best at a table, I believe. We talked about ceviche, pancreatitis, and the beautiful, hyperviolent plays of British-Irish playwright Martin McDonagh. Shit devolved. We got in the car and listened to the Who on the way home. Everyone sang along. The Doors came on next.

"Were you into the Doors?" I asked.

"Yeah, I got the first Doors forty-five," Julian said.

"Did you eat acid?" Ed asked, laughing.

"Naw," Julian said. "'Hello, I Love You' was the first stereo forty-five, and I had it."

"What's the first band you saw live?" I asked.

"Probably the Beach Boys or the Stones," Julian said.

He loves the Rolling Stones, which must have driven his tank captain father absolutely nuts. "They've been here several times," Julian said. "I saw them from the parking lot at the old Cardinal Stadium at the fairgrounds. I saw them at Churchill Downs."

We got home. The party wasn't over. We were at the best bar in the world: Julian's house. As a rule, I always let him pick what we're drinking. It feels rude to start shot-calling: *Uh, yeah, can you get some Stitzel-Weller white dog from when your granddad ran the place? Maybe a 1964 Old Fitz? Maybe some 20-year-old Pappy?*

Tonight he pulled out a barrel-aged Nicaraguan rum he likes. If he was going rum, then we were following suit, on the rocks with a twist of lemon. Ed got a guitar and we passed it around. He played a beautiful version of Widespread Panic's "Space Wrangler."

We drove around the neighborhood on a golf cart, then we dropped Julian off and started talking about getting guns to "shoot shit." Ed played Widespread's "Driving Song," which always leaves me melancholy and nostalgic:

> *The leaves seen through my window pane*
> *Remind me that it's time to move my life again.*

We drove the cart onto a highway overpass. I leaned out over the concrete railing and looked down. Cars rushed beneath our feet, and the tires whined below in a blur of white and red lights. That's when Ed started talking about Julian. He told me the real story of Lawrenceburg.

All those years out in the wilderness, Julian wasn't breaking even. He went close to a million dollars in debt, taking out loans, spending through his inheritance, doing whatever it took to keep Old Rip in bottles and in stores. The whiskey business cost him nearly everything and yet he endured. And he wasn't waiting for a boom. He didn't see the future. That would make him a genius but would also somehow cheapen how far he was willing to go to put out another year of bourbon. Julian is a man willing to go down with the ship.

"This story has got to be told," Ed said, "because it's not like he was Pappy's son and he had it made and he just fell into this. He was beating the machines with a wrench to make them operate. You've gotta talk to Aunt Sally about it. Aunt Sally was the one telling stories the other night about him in the flood, standing on top of the thing, beating it with a wrench. She told it last night. You've gotta have those stories. It's rags to fucking riches. He's spent all the money from the sale of the distillery keeping it alive and trying not to drop out of the country club where he'd grown up. They didn't have any money. Fucking peanut butter and jelly at the club. Sissy will tell you, she'd take the kids out to the car to eat sandwiches and bring them back into the pool. This thing didn't just happen overnight, and my biggest respect for Julian is that . . . man, I get it."

I thought about Julian asleep up the hill. He grew up in the house next door to the one where he lives now. His entire adult life has been in the shadow of what his family built and lost. I think about the ultimate Southern act: the keeping up of appearances.

During some lean years as a boy and a young man, my own family did the same thing. Something Preston Van Winkle told me came to mind. Julian loves these big cans of Hubs Virginia peanuts a friend mailed him every year for Christmas—"like, guarded them with his life," Preston said—and after a long day out in Lawrence-burg, Julian used to love coming home and pouring a drink and eating the peanuts. Or, he'd come home and mow the yard with an ice-cold can of Budweiser, a pattern his son would find himself emulating as a grown man, and then he'd come in to eat his peanuts. And he would always share them with Preston. In the moment, Preston didn't understand how much weight his father carried on his shoulders. That was his takeaway. Not the peanuts. But that his dad was under tremendous pressure and yet somehow never allowed that to be communicated to his only son, who adored him. "As busy as he was trying to keep the lights on in the eighties and nineties," Preston said, "he always made time for me. Whether it was playing basketball, throwing the football or baseball, or going to sporting events and the like. We went to tons of minor league baseball, soccer, and ice hockey games. Air shows, tractor pulls, and monster truck rallies. We'd go out to my uncle's piece of property and shoot oranges with shotguns and pistols and find vines to swing on. Because he always made sure to make time, it didn't occur to me until later how hard he was busting his ass to keep things afloat."

I looked back up at the darkened house on the hill. I could imagine Preston and Julian crowded over the big can of peanuts. I could see Julian's children playing with the other kids at the country club pool and then skipping the expensive chicken tenders for a homemade sandwich in the car. I could see Julian with bank statements, or going into the bank to get another loan, or moving money around to keep his whiskey on the shelves. He did all of that and then he made it out the other side.

NOW HE WAS BACK.

Julian and his son stood out front of the black haunted house of a bottling plant, overgrown and with the Salt River running through the back. They walked around the side, taking it all in. We were in Appalachia, if not geographically then certainly spiritually. The place gave off a serious no-fucking-trespassing vibe.

"We might get shot," Julian said.

"This guy is definitely armed and doesn't like strangers," I said.

"Don't you think we should tell him we're here before we go snooping around?" Preston asked.

We walked back around to the front and stepped inside. The place was full, floor to ceiling, with enormous and intricate signs, one in the shape of a guitar and another in the shape of a piano. It was a madcap workshop, cavernous and packed with all kinds of leftover electronics and machinery.

A man approached.

Julian stuck out his hand.

"Julian Van Winkle."

The man clocked the name.

"Lou Defino," he said.

"I drove by a few months ago and no one was here," Julian said.

"Well, there's definitely some history here, isn't there?" Lou replied. Lou told him that the old tanks and bottling line have been sold to a guy who set up a distillery up the Highway 151. He thought about hanging on to them but decided he'd rather have the cash and be rid of the headache and the temptation.

"I'm getting old," Defino said. "I'm seventy-one years old and I still work every day with my hands; get tired and hot. You may know of him. Three Boys Distillery, the name is."

Julian recognized the name. "We saw him yesterday at Buffalo Trace," he said. "I signed some decanters for his three grandchildren."

The coincidence felt eerie; he met some upstart bourbon guy inspired by the boom Julian helped create, and that guy bought the same old bottling line that Julian fought and wrestled all those years ago. I could feel Julian's metabolism change, suddenly open to the cosmic ideas floating around above us. The confluence of meeting the guy who bought his old bottling line, and then being forced by me to come out here and see the building where it once rattled away day after day, year after year, it was almost like this part of his life was stalking him, forcing him to reckon with these things.

Lou explained the barrel brands he'd found down in the dirt, and old bottles, and all manner of remnants of the whiskey making that once happened here. Julian left me and Preston to carry the conversation while he wandered around in a daze, finding his old fire extinguisher with his name still on the registration plate. The building looked different, but it was familiar enough to take him back to a place he didn't like to go.

"There's my old tow-motor," Julian said.

He turned to Lou.

"Still working?"

Lou nodded.

Preston stared at the mobile lift.

"I can't believe that thing is still around and still working," he said.

"So you used to work here?" Lou asked Preston.

"My sisters and I used to ride that thing around," he said.

There were so many memories out here that when Julian drifted away from the conversation with Lou, it was clear he'd gotten lost in his own past. His kids grew up out here as he kept the business alive. They called the winding highway to the plant the Roller Coaster Road. Julian would accelerate over the hills in his Honda Accord and the bottom would drop out from the kids' stomachs. They grew up smelling whiskey just like he did. While he worked, they'd play in the Salt River, or slide down the box chute, or drive down to the warehouse in the old truck. Carrie loves stories about them going into work with their dad. "Some of our favorite memories were down at the bottling plant," she told me. "We'd get to pack a lunch and eat chips and Doritos and get Cokes out of the vending machine. We'd 'surf' on the conveyor belt, make the push forklift a ride toy, play down in the creek and find salamanders and crawdads and put them on Dad's steering wheel for when it was time to go home. We did like the part where we rolled the barrels off the truck and into the dump room, banged the bungs out, and spilled the whiskey into the filter. We'd climb the ladder to the top of the tank and take a big whiff of the preproofed whiskey. We loved the smell and it will always remind me of Lawrenceburg."

Those were some of the memories rushing back to Julian as he stood around and half-listened to Lou tell stories. Finally he emerged from his own world, looking into the guts of the towmotor to see how Lou had it wired and powered. It was starting to occur to him that Lou was a kind of genius.

"I'll be damned," Julian said. "It's got four golf cart batteries in there. Six volt. Man, that's bad to the bone."

"They don't make anything even close to that now," Lou said. "It's fast and it'll pick up four thousand pounds just like that."

We realized pretty quickly that Lou not only worked in the dilapidated building, he lived there, too. I hope he doesn't ever read this, because I don't want to be rude, but the place had a horror movie vibe to me. Like, I would never, ever come out here alone and unarmed. And that doesn't even take into account the rats and raccoons and all manner of creepy crawlies who'd taken up residence in parts of the building not occupied by Lou and his lady friend.

"Every once in a while you'll hear them sounds," Lou said, "but I'm cool with it."

"So you're living where the bottling room was?" Julian asked.

"No," Lou said. "Actually, you see that little porch up there, under the door right there. . . . I'm in that little storage room."

"Yeah, that's where the bottled whiskey, we would store it," Julian said.

A backwoods Narnia awaited. If you ran a militia, it would be your dream home. Lou led us through a small door into the apartment he'd built himself out of nothing. The creative engineering on display was incredible. He'd insulated it and built walls where none existed and had a couch and a television and a bed and everything they needed to live.

"Julian, that's what I wanted you to see," Defino said. "I threw plywood on that and studded the walls and insulated them and made me a little trap door to where I could go out and around."

It looked like something built by a hillbilly Robinson Crusoe or a mountain holler Swiss Family Robinson, such a strange combination of slapdash amateur make-do-ism combined with a real frontier proficiency.

"That is amazing," Julian said. "This guy is handier than a pocket in a shirt."

"This does not compute," Preston said.

Something else occurred to me, looking from Julian and Preston to Lou and back again. No matter how polished Julian seemed now, he once lived Lou's life, out in this holler on a backwoods road. Lou's day-to-day grind was once Julian's. Julian remembered a few times when he actually said a prayer to his dead father, asking for help. There were a lot of low moments he left buried out here, or at least he thought he did. During his time in Lawrenceburg, he'd grown further away from Pappy and a lot closer than he cared to admit to Lou.

Defino snapped us back to the conversation.

"Julian, are you still at Buffalo?" he asked.

"Yeah, it's going well," Julian said.

"You bottlin' your whiskey?" Defino asked.

"Yeah, they are making it, bottling it, everything," Julian said. "It's a good deal. I came out well on that, as far as not having to do all this shit anymore."

Defino smiled. He understood. "Johnny Cash said, 'If you put the screws to me I'm gonna screw right out the bottom of it,'" he said with a laugh.

- 18 -

THIS IS WHERE JULIAN WAS WORKING when he got the call that would change his life. This is where he stopped being a guy like Lou and started to become some sort of cultural icon. He remembers the phone call perfectly. It was from a woman named Patty. She worked at what is now Diageo and called to tell Julian that they had excess whiskey for sale. The company was unloading its bourbon: from shutting down the Stitzel-Weller plant to shedding its famous brands to trying to find buyers for the barrels in its warehouses. The big corporation didn't know what it had; it got rid of the old machines and Pappy's living yeast. Bourbon was part of its past, and so these barrels needed to go. They were priced as low as $200 each. For an entire barrel. Julian flipped page after page and wondered why an enormous corporation with lawyers and accountants and vice presidents and meetings and conference calls didn't see the same value he saw on those pages. Until then, Julian had been buying barrels from the Old Boone distillery and bottling that as Old Rip Van Winkle. Every now and then he'd get some barrels of Stitzel-Weller and put them out under a special label, including the best whiskey I've ever personally tasted, sitting at his kitchen island, a 1968 distillation that was bottled as Family Reserve in 1984. Bourbon heads will recognize the label as being nearly similar to the one he uses now for the Van Winkle rye.

Patty needed to move product. In hindsight, United Distillers took a huge bank vault of money and lit it on fire. The truth is, nobody understood what they had given up and what, in those thousands of barrels they were using as part of the Crown Royal blend, they still had. But Julian did. That was the taste of his youth, and the last pieces he could hold of his father and grandfather. Fine, aged wheated bourbon was his family's legacy—that's what he was really trying to protect. "Of course I believed in it because it was really good," he said. "That's when I got excited, because I tasted that whiskey. I was bottling Old Boone and all this other shit. I tasted the Stitzel-Weller stuff that Master Distiller Ed Foote was making since we sold the distillery and it was awesome."

Looking at this list of barrels, he knew what he needed to do. Each barrel, depending on evaporation, was good for ten to eighteen cases of whiskey. He called a local banker looking for a loan, offering the stock he'd inherited from his father as collateral. The first banker refused, saying these barrels weren't worth the money they'd have to loan Julian to buy them. Finally, after making his case, he got someone to extend him a line of credit and he began buying up as many barrels as he could afford. In the bottling of it he felt he should pay respect to his family and to the distillery that made this beautiful whiskey, so he named his brand Van Winkle Family Reserve and put Pappy's picture on the label. "The first year we bottled the 20-year-old it was awesome," Julian said, "and I was like making eggnog with 20-year-old Pappy. I felt really guilty but boy it was really good eggnog. I had cases of this stuff sitting around and it was so good. I couldn't believe how good it was, because this was 20-year-old Stitzel-Weller bourbon not stored on a top floor, but the cooler floors. We don't have anything like that anymore because it's gone."

That's how it happened. He survived. Being in Lawrenceburg with Julian is so powerful and hard to explain, because his relief at his survival pours off him. His father ran out of time, same as mine, but this place is where Julian made his own time. He'd held on long enough for someone to come looking for a man who always makes fine bourbon, at a profit if he can, at a loss if he must . . . but always fine bourbon.

Pappy came out and got a perfect 99-score review from the Beverage Testing Institute in 1996, which named it the greatest bourbon in the world. Here's one last bit of myth busting: although Julian created Pappy as a vehicle for that Stitzel-Weller, a bourbon bottler never ever wastes juice, so the liquor in that famous bottle rated a 99 wasn't the Stitzel-Weller but some of the Old Boone that was left over. He needed to finish up the last of that before getting to the truly transcendent stuff. So Julian is one of the few people who knows that Pappy got that first 99 and then the really great whiskey started to come out in the bottles bearing the picture of his granddad. Julian stayed out in the wilderness until he made a bourbon that caught the public's imagination, and six years and dozens of barrels of Stitzel-Weller later, Buffalo Trace called and offered to buy into his brand and Julian left Lawrenceburg forever. His success made me think about my dad, and his dad, who both ran out of time, and about Julian, who'd endured—*who made his own time*—and found through his work and struggle the life-giving forces that eluded his father. He made the trip. He made it for both of them.

PEOPLE DON'T TREAT JULIAN LIKE A CELEBRITY. I've been around celebrities. There's a different kind of respect for him. Supplicants want an audience more than proof of life. He doesn't inspire selfies as much as handshakes. We sat courtside at a University of Kentucky basketball game, directly behind Coach Cal, who screamed at his players during one tense time-out, "This isn't high school!" As Julian and I peered around the assistants to follow the action, a man walked over and gathered his nerve and said, tentatively, "Mr. Van Winkle?"

Julian smiled and took the man's hand.

"I'm a big fan of your bourbon," the man said and then excused himself, having delivered the message that pulled him from his seat and sent him down past the scorer's table to the Kentucky bench. A few minutes later, Julian saw a woman he knew in the stands with her new baby and after he waved big, he leaned over to me, grinned, and said, "Future customer."

This is the life that started for him after Pappy. "The cult bourbon shit," Julian called it. I've seen the madness up close, again and again. Not long after our day in Lawrenceburg, Julian, Preston, and I went out to San Francisco for WhiskyFest. We stood behind their table and waited for the hordes to descend. Every age of Pappy was on the table in front of us, and then the doors opened and the line wound around the whole hotel ballroom. Someone wanted the 24-year-old, which doesn't exist. Julian chuckled and said, "We've got 23, 20, and 15."

"You're saving the 24-year-old for yourself," the guy said.

People lined up and got a small pour of whiskey and a photo and a few words. The first bottle of 23-year-old was gone in six minutes. I was counting. Someone asked for the empty bottle. Preston politely told him no and, when nobody was looking, scratched the label so people couldn't sell it online full of cheap whiskey. Eight minutes later, the second and final bottle of 23-year-old was gone. People would be lined up for hours. A few liquor store owners got aggressive with Julian and Preston about how much they were sent every year. "How is it I spend so much money, and I don't have enough allocation?" a man asked. "How do I get more allocation?"

That is the question that follows the Van Winkles around the bourbon world, and nobody wants to hear the real answer: they have no say over who gets their whiskey or over how much retailers charge for it. Julian is forever raging about how the state liquor boards control the allocations. In New York, for instance, he can't even make sure that Eleven Madison Park, a Michelin-starred restaurant that has supported his whiskey since before it was cool, gets as much as it wants. The whole thing feels corrupt. Ed is always checking price tags and complaining to store owners about their outrageous markups. Once he ordered Pappy at a bar near a ski resort and what they poured out of the bottle was not Pappy. They told him he was wrong. He asked to see the manager. The manager asked how he could tell. Ed explained his connection. The manager said he'd check and never returned. The next day, the bottles were gone.

Sometimes shit happens *at* the plant. A few years ago, a bunch of whiskey went missing from the distillery itself. The local papers called it Pappygate. A loading dock employee stole around $100,000 of whiskey that he worked to sell through a syndicate made up of members of his rec-league softball team. The bottle scam feels like the kind of small detail that could serve as the opening metaphor in a book about the fall of the American republic. This ham-fisted minor league Cornbread Mafia also trafficked in guns and steroids.

A law enforcement whiskey enthusiast stopped by the table in San Francisco. Everywhere Julian went, people wanted to talk about the stolen whiskey.

"Do you mind me asking," the cop said, "I recently read that with the recent convictions with everyone that's pled with the bourbon heist, how did that affect your company and how things are going?"

Julian smiled thinly. "We were selling everything we had before the robbery, and we're selling everything we have after the robbery," he said. "So all it did was make the supplies that much tighter and now people hear about us because of the robbery and they want to get some of the whiskey, and it makes it even harder to find, so it makes things worse for you all."

As I took in the event, I realized I'm seeing the same scene playing out over and over again. Some people were real asshats. The whole thing caused a visceral reaction that caught me off guard. It didn't make sense or even reflect the overall spirit of the event. Most people were lovely and sharing a bucket list experience with friends, and yet I hated to admit that the longer I stood here the more I focused on the asshats. It was strange and exhausting. An idea floated around my subconscious, stubbornly refusing to cohere enough to acquire the power of language, but there was some chain of unintended consequences going on here to create both this event and my reaction to it. Bourbon became popular again, and then it became expensive and rare, which made it more popular and yet so hard to get that its original purpose as a way to facilitate and lubricate fellowship was being replaced by the hunting for and finding of it. The economy of bourbon was pushing out what I loved most about it. Maybe that's why I was reacting so strongly. When the event finally ended, Julian and Preston looked wiped out. They both needed a drink.

"Where you wanna go?" I asked.

"Someplace nearby," Julian said. "Somewhere with good vodka. I'm getting tired of all this whiskey."

We both laughed. It was time to fade into the night and for me to consider what all I'd seen.

I'd always thought that bourbon was a tool. At WhiskyFest it felt like something people wanted to possess. That was weird to me. You drink expensive bourbon and then you piss it out. No getting around that. It's just passing through. While it's in your system, if you don't drink too much of it and try to start a fight or some shit, that's where the brief, flickering magic happens. Whiskey warms your insides and not just literally. There didn't seem like a lot of warming going on in San Francisco, just a pelt-hunting mad dash.

One night at the Van Winkles' house, I got on my high horse about how ridiculous I found the fetishizing of whiskey, the way it is turned into the event itself as opposed to either a lubricant for the event or a way to shine a light on the unspoken meaning of an event. I was trashing the festivalgoers and both Julian and Sissy politely scolded me. People should be able to express their passion for something they love in whatever way they want, and the communities brought together by people who drink and discuss whiskey were no less valid than those where people drink whiskey and discuss baseball or politics or military history. I was being a snob and imposing my own values and biases onto other people. If they'd learned anything touring the world serving Pappy—Sissy worked those first events with Julian, before anyone had ever heard of them or wanted to buy a bottle—it was the knowledge that there were always a few jackasses but that they were usually outshone by the people who came to meet them, and to try a taste, with an earnest intention, with real pureness of heart.

They've seen a tribe spring up around their whiskey, seen many tribes, really: those who buy it as a status symbol, those who can't find it and long for it, those who can't find it and blame everyone and especially them for that inability. It was an odd and beautiful thing to behold, more like seeing the northern lights than a strong brand culture. To explain, Sissy told me a story about a whiskey festival in New York years ago.

There was this guy, a doctor, a small, gentle man who had brought his father and friends to WhiskyFest. They really hit it off, laughing, as he got to the front of the line. His name was Elliot Goldofsky. Then, later, she ran into him again, with all his friends, and as he introduced her, they told her he was the best otolaryngologist in America. She asked what on earth that meant. Everyone laughed. Sissy and Elliot got to talking, first about surface things like bourbon, and then later, about really important things like life. At one point he blurted, "I feel so strongly we were meant to meet this evening."

She went home. A week later, she and Julian found out their young son, Preston, was partially deaf. Now, four decades later, sitting at their dinner table in Kentucky, she began to cry. She cried then, too, she said, and went back into the story. They'd exchanged information and she found his number and called up to New York. Her voice broke when he answered.

"Elliot," she said. "I need you."

She smiled at me. Tears were still in her eyes. Elliot helped them choose the doctor who operated on Preston to try to restore his hearing. Now Preston will be the one to carry on those traditions and share them with people like a random doctor who came out to get a drink with some friends.

- 20 -

JULIAN LEFT THE CORN ON THE GRILL and came to greet me at the door. I'd finally taken the Van Winkles up on their offer to visit their "camp" in Michigan, which for me conjured visions of some rustic deer hunting place. When I followed the map to Harbor Springs, Michigan, and found huge white mansions on the shore and a quaint downtown like something from the Hamptons, I started to laugh. Victorian summer homes with wide porches and American flags looked out onto rolling lawns and flower beds. Narrow footpaths ran between the homes, the whole place idyllic and languid. Old industrialist money lives up here on this lake—and new money, too: Betsy DeVos's Amway-funded ship is at anchor in the marina. Pappy started to vacation here in the 1930s, even before he opened Stitzel-Weller. I came into a great room with a cathedral ceiling flooded with light.

"First of all," Julian said, "what would you like?"

"I'd like a glass of water and then a whiskey drink."

They built this house in the past decade for their ever-expanding family of grandkids (there is a huge bunk room upstairs laid out like in the children's book *Madeline*), able to afford such a place because of the success of Pappy. For years, they piled into small condos or rented houses and scrimped and saved and kept this vestige of Pappy's genteel old world alive and part of their tradition. Now they'd built this big home, with enough room for everyone, and during the summer they pack up from the swelter of Kentucky and the family circles through. Pappy's real value to his family can't be seen at whiskey shows or on bourbon blogs. The success bought him the space and freedom to have this life and the luxury of having all his people close and along for the ride. They live slow here. I liked it. He poured drinks. Music played. We sat around and talked, and although I thought he was blissed out, there was something churning just out of sight.

"Lawrenceburg, Kentucky," he said, apropos of nothing. "Did that hit you heavy like it hit me? That was a freaky day."

I was surprised he wanted to go back there. I told him that was the first time I really understood what Pappy meant to him. I'd always seen his bourbon as an inheritance story, not a survival-in-the-wilderness story. "That's probably the most important part about this whole thing," he said, "that fucking awful but blessed thing that kicked this whole thing off from 1983 until 2002."

"If someone would have told you in 1988 that you were going to have the most sought after and deified bourbon in the world, you would have looked at them like they were smoking crack."

He laughed.

"Nah," he said. "We were just trying to make a bank payment next week."

"How close did you come really?" I asked.

He told me a story.

"Wequetonsing, where we were tonight," he said. "I remember one summer walking down there, probably mideighties, when I used to buy whiskey from Wild Turkey, Old Boone distillation that they were putting in Wild Turkey, and Wild Turkey said, 'Nope, we can't sell you any more whiskey this year.' I remember walking down that sidewalk towards the lake to our rental house, which is on the left, one house off the lake, most beautiful views. Beautiful deck, looking out towards the harbor and I'm going okay, 'This is the last summer I'm coming up here. I'm done.'"

"What happened?"

"I guess something came available," he said. "It was scary."

There was a lesson in there somewhere, about stubbornness or confidence or belief. He said he didn't ever think about hitting it big, or if he was letting his father and grandfather down. The daily struggle of keeping it open kept existential fears at bay. "I was gonna ride this thing into the grave," he said, "because it was all I knew how to do. I was spending. Thankfully I had a bunch of stock my dad had given me and I just kept kind of spending that to keep it alive."

- 21 -

THAT NIGHT IN MICHIGAN, the sun slid down on another perfect day, and I couldn't even really tell you what we did besides get a sandwich and some chips and a few beers, and ride out on a boat on a lake that looks like glass, and come back to the house to brainstorm what at the butcher shop might taste good on the grill, and whether or not we can get ourselves together enough to make peach ice cream. Sonia had flown up to hang out, too. It was a perfect evening.

But first, a cocktail. These were vital decisions.

"Thinking about what I want to put in my body," Julian said.

The weather was perfect, maybe a little too hot but nothing a sunset and some booze wouldn't cure. Julian wore shorts and a turquoise shirt.

"I'm thinking about a margarita and I'm thinking about making a Vanhattan," he said.

"I always want a Vanhattan," I told him.

A Vanhattan is his personal riff on a Manhattan.

"I don't want you to open a bottle just for—"

"I'm not opening nothing," he interrupted, and then went over to the kitchen, looking for fruit. "I think we got an orange at the grocery."

"What's in a Vanhattan?" I asked as he started to mix.

"It's half rye, half bourbon," he said.

When he said rye, he meant the Van Winkle rye. And when he said bourbon, he meant Pappy. The bar was on the wall near the grill. He poured from feel; he didn't need jiggers.

"Carpano Antica vermouth," he said.

He spooned in juice from a jar of Luxardo cherries.

"How much?"

"About two teaspoons," he said. "Just kind of do it to taste. It's about the same with the Carpano Antica."

He reached for a small bottle on the bar. A few steps were left before cocktail hour could commence. "Two or three shakes of orange bitters or blood orange bitters, which is what I made it with the first time, which is about the same thing but a little more intense," he said. "And a twist of orange that really sets it off."

He finished mixing the drinks and handed me one and kept one for himself. We both had a sip.

"They go down real easy," he said.

Arthur Alexander played on the stereo. We didn't talk much. We didn't really talk at all. There was nothing that needed to be said. He smiled. "See, I want another one of those but it's straight whiskey," he said. "This is kind of like lemonade to me, it just goes down kind of nice, sweet, and fast. Very dangerous."

"I think you should have another one."

"I think I probably should, too."

Julian pulled out a bottle of wine, a Spanish Meritage, made from Monastrell and Syrah variety of grapes, aged in Pappy Van Winkle barrels with their good friend Dan Philips. The color of the wine was this beautiful almost unnaturally bright red. The land where these grapes are born sits by the Segura River, bracketed by two mountain ranges in a part of Spain settled by the Moors. We went outside and threw the ball with his dog. Sissy chopped three cloves of garlic for the polenta and added some bacon grease to the greens cooking on the stove. They grew the greens themselves. Sonia and Sissy talked about jewelry. Julian put on "Purple Rain" and turned up the volume. Something about the melancholy fat guitar chords made it feel like a cosmic sibling to bourbon. Julian disappeared to his liquor cabinet and came back with tumblers of bourbon on the rocks with a lemon twist. He wanted me to guess what was in the glass, and after I fumbled around, he smiled.

"I put a twist of lemon in it," he said. "It makes it better. I'm not sure you've ever had that. Did you like this? It's Maker's Mark made in the late eighties."

"How much Maker's Mark from the late eighties do you have?"

"A bottle and a half in there and my buddy down the road has about a bottle of it," he said. "We found it in a house that we rented years ago, while we were building this house. They had bottles and bottles of Maker's Mark in there, and I tasted an open bottle and I looked at the bottom and it said 1992 or something, which was when the bottle was made, so it was made in the eighties and it's just so beyond what they're making now. I bought a couple of bottles from the owner."

"Did they change the recipe?" Sonia asked.

"Oh yeah, they did," Julian said. "There are so few bottles like these left on earth."

This was their life. A perfect drink, poured from a found bottle of old-school Maker's Mark. The seductive Van Winkle thing is really a series of mostly replicable actions and details and moments. You could live this life if you wanted. That's real peace, I think. They love each other. It's impossible to miss, in the way Sissy looks at him across a table after all these years, in the way he always takes the juiciest or best piece of anything he grills and brings it to her on a fork. He's got a telescope powerful enough to see the rings on Saturn. Pointing it up at the sky gives him a limitless feeling. She tends a vegetable garden. Sometimes she'll cut flowers. Both of them read books. Sissy likes to paddle her kayak and do Pilates. Julian swims out to the buoy where he keeps their boat and motors around the lake. Growing up with their own kids, their boat was known to everyone as *The Gofasterdaddy*. All the children in the neighborhood wanted Mr. Julian to pull them in an inner tube. Now their grandkids smile from pictures hanging all over the house.

Long ago Sissy decided no bunk beds for the kids. They're a

bitch to make up, she says. Julian got a full-size urinal installed, with a brass bar above it in case anyone gets a little wobbly. There's also a marble shelf for a cocktail. He knows a knife-maker who works with Damascus steel. He makes his own Kahlúa. Sissy plays mah-jongg. Julian listens to Alan Jackson. Once their triplets all got arrested for Walking Under the Influence. They thought that was hilarious. The paper printed the infraction: CARRIE AND LOU-ISE AND CHENAULT VAN WINKLE FROM LOUISVILLE, KENTUCKY WERE ARRESTED.

Both of them love the willow trees. Bikes hang from the ceiling and walls of the garage. Everyone travels the town by bike. Julian's wrecked at least twice. "Embarrassing," he said, smiling. "Over-served. One night I was looking at the moon and the town had just put up those big speed machines that had your speed on it, eight feet tall, only it was turned off. I nailed that thing. I have a scar here where it looks like I had lung surgery. Broke a rib, I'm sure, maybe a couple of them. Big scar, and just embarrassing. I've had a couple of them, but it's part of the game. . . ."

We sat out on the porch under the light of flickering candles. The music filtered through the air.

What became clear in Michigan was that Julian and Sissy have become the fully realized version of themselves through success. That's actually rare. I profile famous and successful athletes for a living and almost no one understands that success is merely a cur-rency to spend on one big purchase. Do you use it to try to get more success? To maintain the attention and bright lights? Or do you buy a life with it? The kind of life most people really want. I wanted what they have, wanted to organize the next act of my life, the one that moved finally past my youthful dreams and the rage and ambition that come shaped and fueled by my most broken and insecure self. The same questions from earlier returned. What does a man owe his father? What does he owe his younger self? Does a man lose whatever is left of his spirit when the last Stitzel-Weller is gone?

"Is anybody sitting on a huge supply?" I asked.

"Not anymore," he said.

"When will the last barrel be bottled?"

"It may have already been bottled," he said.

- 22 -

SONIA AND I LEFT THE VAN WINKLES and headed north toward
Lake Superior, the tires making a rumbling noise on the highway.
We rode in silence, looking at the roadside diners and thinking.
The coming baby changed all our calculus, and I found myself no
longer trying to escape but now moving with just as much urgency
toward a home where I could leave the running behind. I thought
of the Chief Joseph quote: I will fight no more forever. Our destination was a small town in the Upper Peninsula of Michigan and the
waterfront compound owned by my friend and mentor Rick
Telander.

I had an important question to ask.

Sonia's pregnancy was progressing perfectly, the doctors assured
us, but we still felt anxious and uncertain, and as long as we didn't
tell a lot of people, or didn't start planning for a birth, or outfitting

our house for a third human who would be living there, then we were somehow protected against heartbreak. There'd been so much of that—I still cannot shake the twenty-four hours surrounding a miscarriage in Paris—and so, after such a long and oftentimes bleak journey, we wanted to protect this miracle of a baby girl, whom we'd decided to name Wallace after my grandfather—my mom's dad, William Wallace McKenzie.

I wanted Rick to be Wallace's godfather.

There was a chain at work here. I first met Rick at the Super Bowl in Atlanta. He was a famous writer, formerly of *Sports Illustrated* and now of the *Chicago Sun-Times*. His most famous book is a classic called *Heaven Is a Playground*. My friends Seth, Justin, Steve, and I had somehow managed to get credentials to cover the game for our student newspaper. Seth, who started and fueled our magazine story obsession, knew about Rick before I did. He's the one who recognized Rick, and over that week, we drank with him and played pickup basketball with him. I kept in touch. Rick was the first person to really believe in me. He taught valuable writing lessons. In one, he used the second verse of Bruce Springsteen's "Hungry Heart."

> *I met her in a Kingstown bar*
> *We fell in love I knew it had to end*
> *We took what we had and we ripped it apart*
> *Now here I am down in Kingstown again*

There are thirty-five words in those lyrics. Four have more than one syllable. And yet the verse tells a huge arc of human desire and loneliness and loss. That's writing, he said. Be simple, blunt, and profound. The lessons opened the songbook to me. Springsteen's characters in his songs struggled with the same fears and obstacles as I do. So I listened to those records over and over again. *Darkness on the Edge of Town* became my origin document at a critical moment in my career. The stories on that recording center around familiar characters in the Springsteen universe, but they all feel autobiographical to me given what I know of the professional and creative challenges Bruce faced in that part of his life. The album *Born to Run* had taken the musical world by force—he'd famously been on the covers of *Time* and *Newsweek* at the same time—and yet his contract kept him from cashing in and controlling his own ship. He went to war, fighting for his freedom while risking this fragile embryo of a career. He had no way to look decades into the future to see what lay in store for him. He risked his dream to actually own his dream, and for three years, he couldn't record or release any music; left to write the songs on *Darkness* and stew. To me, it's a record about trying to protect a dream while confronted with a growing wall of reality that says the dream is dead—and worse: useless, pathetic, impossible.

Men walk through these gates with death in their eyes. Some folks are born into a good life. Other folks, they just get it any way anyhow. You're born into this life paying for the sins of somebody else's past.

You're born with nothing and better off that way. Soon as you've got something they send someone to try and take it away. You inherit the sins, you inherit the flames. Some guys they just give up living and start dying little by little, piece by piece. You wake up in the night with a fear so real. I'm caught in a cross fire that I don't understand. Sometimes I feel so weak I just want to explode. When we found the things we loved, they were crushed and dying in the dirt. I packed my bags and I'm heading straight into the storm. Gonna be a twister to blow everything down that ain't got the faith to stand its ground. Everybody's got a hunger, a hunger they can't resist. Poor man wanna be rich. Rich man wanna be king. I've been working real hard, trying to get my hands clean. Let the broken hearts stand as the price you've gotta pay. Tonight I'll be on that hill 'cause I can't stop. I'll be there on time and I'll pay the cost.

Those themes never left Springsteen's music or his life. He has said his goal with his own family was to avoid the pain inflicted on him by his father, to be, as he put it, an ancestor in their lives and not a ghost. He wanted to walk by their side and guide and protect, not grasp their ankles and pull them back down. That feels like a choice to me. You decide the story to tell about yourself—the myth that enables you to strive and hope to be your best self. My father, then, is an ancestor, not a ghost. Willie Morris is an ancestor, not a ghost, and Rick Telander is, like the other important men in my life, also an ancestor and not a ghost. All our influences—mentors and novelists and songwriters—walk with us on the road, not offering advice so much as helping us to unlock the best of ourselves that hides in places we can't otherwise find. That's the work of adulthood. Sorting out the good and bad within. That's the conflict I kept running into: Myth is both the deliverance and the curse. We tell ourselves a story to survive and then that story consumes us, destroys us. The mask eats the face. That's an Updike quote that my friend Scott told me, and I've been using it ever since to talk about the athletes I profile.

- 23 -

I WAS BORN IN A MASK, the monk and philosopher Thomas Merton wrote. He lived and wrote in a monastery in Kentucky, and while I worked on understanding Julian and saw the miracle of our daughter coming into existence, I also began to read lots of Merton, trying to make sense of how my need to run was being replaced by a desire to stay. All my running felt like a mask. Bourbon, especially status-cult bourbon, is a mask, too. It's something put on to hide or amplify. Pappy isn't my mask, but I definitely wear them. ESPN is a mask. A book on *The New York Times* bestseller list is a mask. Merton is aiming his critique at himself and at everyone who has ever strived for anything. And what is Pappy if not the result of striving sold mostly to strivers? *Our being is not to be enriched by activity and experience as such. Everything depends on the quality of our acts and our experiences. . . . We are so obsessed with doing that we have no time and no imagination left for being.*

Ontonagon, Michigan, is a remote dive-bar town. Places of community, communion, and shit-kicking rumbles upon occasion. Newcomers get made immediately. All the bars have great signs. Neon soothes loneliness. We made our way down dark roads until we found the Telander compound. That's what it is, too. A main house, on the beach. A stand-alone sauna. A big barn with his woodshop and a bunk room upstairs. A few small houses for his grown children to stay when they come to visit. We turn into the drive. The house is full of Telanders, who welcome us into their big, beautiful, strange tribe.

Sonia was only in her second trimester. The pregnancy was new. I don't think she fully believed. I know I didn't. The memory of her miscarriage scarred us both. I will never forget her walking out of the doctor's office at the American Hospital of Paris on Boulevard Victor Hugo and just shaking her head. I cried ugly tears on our balcony that day and neither of us thought we'd ever get to have a family of our own. At the Telanders', she bonded with Rick's daughters and played games and ate food and listened to stories and told stories. Rick played the guitar. We all sang. Every so often, I'd look over to see Sonia relaxed for the first time in as long as I could remember. Sitting in the Telander compound, we first started to believe.

She saw what Rick had built for his kids and grandkids. Later she told me that a clear and powerful thought came to her then, as she tried to hope our family into being while surrounded by this big, beautiful family created by Rick and Judy. She loved the big

"Telander Beach Club" flag and the pinewood interior that glowed in the amber. Green lights ringed the front porch and the house sounded like music and laughter.

"So this is what it means," she said and I understood. We build a life to share, to pass on, so that some idea of us can live in our children and grandchildren, so that we might live forever and they might never be alone. Sonia and I both felt so hopeful for those few days, finally seeing how it might all manifest for us, if we would just allow ourselves to believe. A place like this is a defiant stand against loneliness, against the idea that we should enter and leave this world as solitary beings. She felt at the Telanders' the same feeling I felt when I first walked into Julian and Sissy's Michigan house, when the absence of a large, loud family didn't mean that the spirits of those people didn't exist as real and sturdy as the beams and walls. . . .

Why, then, do we continue to pursue joys without substance? Merton wrote. *Because the pursuit itself has become our only substitute for joy. Unable to rest in anything we achieve, we determine to forget our discontent in a ceaseless quest for new satisfactions. In this pursuit, desire itself becomes our chief satisfaction.*

That's why I find Julian so intriguing and worthy of respect. He lives and works in the business of selling the myth of his own family to people who long for it in theirs—and not just the whiskey and the cigars and the hats and embroidered belts, but the old over-and-under shotguns and rings and traditions like the Derby and Michigan, the whole gestalt of Van Winkledom, of

Pappyland—and while selling this myth, he doesn't let it consume the actual him at the center of it. That's his greatest gift, I think, and what each bottle I own of Van Winkle represents to me. That's the mask I put on Pappy, which means either I see the bourbon more clearly than anyone else or I'm the biggest sucker of them all.

Do everything to avoid the noise and the business of men.

I have spent two decades obsessed with the noise and business of men, of trying to figure out what my work means, when Merton says it means nothing at all.

Keep as far away as you can from the places where they gather to cheat . . .

The decision to focus on the joy of creation and family instead of ambition lies with me alone.

Be glad if you can keep beyond the reach of their radios.

I feel like some vibrating need has been briefly silenced.

Do not bother with their unearthly songs.

Who do I want to be during the time I have left?

What does Julian want to pass on when he's gone?

Do not read their advertisements.

Pappy Van Winkle was many things: father, husband, honorable businessman, craftsman, wing shot, Derby party host, but perhaps most of all he was an ad man. He could see into the hearts of men and know what they desired and how to sell it to them. All great whiskey barons have that skill in common. And yet, the closer and closer I get to Julian, the more I see someone who isn't trying to sell anyone anything. He'd prefer this book didn't exist, I believe. He'd prefer his whiskey didn't have such an expensive secondary-market price, because that would save him a lot of angry phone calls. He doesn't get any of that markup. What he really cares about is that he lives up to the promise that kept him going all these years—ALWAYS FINE BOURBON—and that promise is not to Pappy or to his father or to Sissy or his children. Julian's whiskey is the public expression of a private promise to himself, a return to the success of his grandfather and, maybe as important, a chance to soothe the pain his father felt when he lost what Pappy had built.

PART III

- 1 -

THERE IS AN ORCHID that lives for only one night. It grows in the wild on cactuses. Old bourbon is a lot like these flowers. Once you crack the seal and pull the cork the whiskey sometimes has only minutes to live. I think of that poem "The Waking" by Theodore Roethke, about how we begin dying the moment we are born. That's true for bourbon, too. One afternoon Julian and I drank an old Stitzel-Weller that had been made in the late 1960s. His father was living when this whiskey got distilled and barreled, and so when he opened the cork—he needed to gently pull it out with a wine key as it crumbled—a world in which his father was still alive briefly filled Julian's kitchen, on our noses and tongues when he poured a glass for each of us. We sat at his kitchen counter and drank in silence.

"This starts to oxidize fast," he said. "Matter of fact, it's already gotten a bit funky."

I couldn't believe how quickly the whiskey changed. The taste Julian loves most and longs to replicate is like one of those desert orchids that flashes beautiful and is gone before the sun.

"It's been open for . . . ," I said.

". . . ten to twenty minutes," he said.

"If that," I said.

"Why is it so sensitive?" he said. "Why is it so fragile?"

- 2 -

THE DAY OF THE TASTING HAD FINALLY ARRIVED, the one that I'd been waiting on since I first started to hang out with Julian. Once more I drove north through rural Mississippi and Tennessee, passing the National Bird Dog Museum about sixty miles east of Memphis. I followed I-65 into Kentucky, passing the National Corvette Museum in Bowling Green. I found myself thinking about how those two museums spoke to each other—a lot of time alone in a car can lead to a lot of theories. It was a solid seven hours from my house to Buffalo Trace.

The tasting that awaited me was the first year that Pappy Van Winkle would be bottled from whiskey made and aged on-site at Buffalo Trace. The juice already poured in glasses with oxidation-proof covers was fifteen years old. Julian's opinion of that whiskey would help determine whether Pappy had a long future or whether it will be one of the many top-shelf brands that come and go like topsoil in a hard wind. That's the unspoken harsh reality in every room where bourbon is made and consumed and discussed.

So many things have changed in the bourbon business since the Stitzel-Weller plant stopped making its flagship bourbon. There is no more Stitzel-Weller. Nobody is making any more and most bourbon experts believe all the old stuff has been used. So all that's left of the greatest bourbon ever made is memory, and the only physical manifestation of that memory lives in Julian's attempt to put out bottles that come close, as he told me a long time ago. He's been chasing the taste and now he'll find out if he's caught it or not. In this business, Julian is a legendary connoisseur, and after all the hype and cult bourbon press and backlash, the expertise he cultivated is what will determine the future of his brand and his business. Those are the stakes. Julian downplayed them, and is probably rolling his eyes as he reads this, but I believe I'm right and I think he agrees with me. That's what I was driving to Buffalo Trace to see. I knew the roads by heart now, turning at the top of the holler and winding my way down toward the water tower that peeks through the trees, built like a shotgun shell with a Coco Chanel wig on top.

When I got out of my car, that familiar smell of corn and young whiskey hit me once again. Smoke rose from the stacks. Heavy machinery jerked and pirouetted to the soundtrack of shrill warning beeps. No matter how romantic you want to make it, a distillery is still an industrial space—a little bit of the rust belt grown up in mountain hollers. There's something magic about that intersection that lives in each bottle. Buffalo Trace claims it's the oldest continuously operating distillery in the country, and that might well be true. It's hard to know when you're talking about whiskey. Maker's Mark claims the same thing—that it occupies the oldest operating bourbon distillery in the world. Here's what I've learned: both are old, and both have been remodeled to look even older, which tells you all you need to know.

Buffalo Trace looks like a theme park from some bygone America, but really, science rules the day. Bourbon is chemistry. This is where Julian or Preston tastes every barrel that ends up in a bottle bearing his family name, looking for off-tasting samples to throw out. We left the gift shop and turned right. It felt like going backstage at a rock show. I never got tired of walking through the distillery with Julian, because even if we didn't talk, he made more sense to me when surrounded by his natural habitat. We passed the brass buffalo surrounded by a small waterfall and pond. Julian looked over to the left. He loved the grassy hill planted with blooming dogwood trees. He'd grown up in a place like this and he always seemed relaxed when surrounded by the familiar sounds and smells, and by the men and women who rushed around him, doing their work. Their continued existence in a changing world seemed to comfort him. A small stream ran down the hill. On the right was a trompe l'oeil painting that depicted the inside of a barrel warehouse. We kept on going until we reached a door. He opened it and we both went inside and the rattling screech of the high-speed bottling line hit us. It was hard to hear.

We went up the back stairs toward the Buffalo Trace lab. The staircase was industrial, the kind of steel girders that connect the decks of a warship. The hall to the lab itself was narrow, and once we were inside, the room felt small and cramped. The science happened here, and the expertise that the marketing department would later sell as magic. Two specially built tables with two different levels of lazy Susans were covered in linoleum to minimize damage from spilled whiskey. None of the staff knew how long the tables have been used. Like a lot of things at a distillery, they predated the longest tenured employee. They'd seen photos of former Master Distiller Elmer T. Lee sitting at the table. He started at the plant in 1949. Several years ago, a local artisan replicated a table when they remodeled the lab. On each lazy Susan sat row upon row of half-pint bottles, each carefully marked, and small wineglasses containing bourbon from each barrel of a particular vintage. A glass coaster rested on top of each one to stop the oxidizing process. Julian had done this maybe a thousand times in his life. Mostly these sessions come and go without much notice being paid. He took a sip and spat the whiskey into a big brass spittoon, no big deal. Everyone, me included, was always stunned at how much great whiskey gets tossed; there was a law against taking these half-pints out of the lab. "I've tasted 23-year-old with someone who didn't spit," Julian said, laughing, "and they almost fainted when I told them we had to throw out what's left over."

- 3 -

MY UNCLE WILL IS THE PATRIARCH OF OUR FAMILY. Not long ago, he brought over a beautiful white dress that was now our turn to have. All the girls in the family had worn it, and he wanted to make sure that tradition continued. He told us the story, how Becky had bought it nearly fifty years ago for their daughter, Susan, to wear to my uncle Michael's wedding. Beautiful and handmade, it came from the Women's Exchange in Memphis. I promised to take care of it and to make sure it got passed to the next little girl to come along. We talked about how impossible it seems that he has a daughter who is more than fifty years old. He smiled and said, "Life isn't designed to stay the same."

Will says things like that a lot. He's funny and fun, with that rare kind of devout faith that attracts people with its promise of peace and an eternal life with God, rather than repels with its dogma and arrogance. He dances at weddings. He cheers for his favorite team without any self-consciousness. His old glory days as a high school football player still work in his memory. When he moved to Yazoo City to set up his medical practice, he started to work for a local high school, Manchester Academy, as the team doctor. A recurring dream began. He'd be wearing the Manchester uniforms, his current age, surrounded by the teenagers, suited up, ready to play a game again. The lights glowed and tiny bugs swarmed the halogen bulbs. His adrenaline spiked and the cheers coming from the metal bleachers echoed inside his helmet, and the noise rose and just before the ball got kicked off to start the game, he woke up. It happened like that every time. He never got to dream about actually playing in the game and eventually the dreams stopped. He's still the team doctor and now gives motivational speeches. Uncle Will loves feeling the radiating energy of their youth and power and remembering when he and my dad played together for Bentonia High School, my dad the quarterback and Will his protective lineman, who'd take on the entire opposing town if he felt like they were attacking his little brother.

In his church, which is much more conservative than I'm comfortable with to be frank, he's led a group that is working through the idea of racial reconciliation. Will is the kind of man who is always open to questions and discovery and debate. That's probably hardwired in him—a mixture of whatever mental acuity drew him to the medical profession and his deep empathy. He now hosts breakfasts at his house with people of different races and political ideologies, so they can walk a mile in one another's shoes. If America had more people like Uncle Will, then we wouldn't be in this mess in which everybody just shouts and sits down in satisfied certitude.

Lately he's gotten into bourbon. I think it's an aging and nostalgia thing. Like Julian, he's been battling cancer, which he's so far kept at bay. But Uncle Will knows he is in the last act of life. There are angels around him now, waiting to take him home to be with his parents and with his brothers. I never knew if he and my dad had ever talked about dying or if they'd ever said goodbye, but after talking to Julian about all the questions he wishes he'd asked his dad, I didn't want to make the same mistake. So I asked Will. He took a day to compose his thoughts and then told me the story. "I never said goodbye," he said, "nor did your daddy. I don't recall ever talking about death with Walter. Not sure why. To me death is not a frightening thing."

My mama and daddy refused to ever give voice to the idea that this might be a losing fight. So Will felt he should respect that warrior spirit. Daddy could hear his high school football coach screaming in his ear across the decades. *You. Are. Not. Gonna. Quit.* So Uncle Will got in line and encouraged as best he could. The closest they ever got was when my mom took my younger brother to college in the last year of Daddy's life. Uncle Will went to stay with Daddy, who had less than a month to live, although we didn't know it then. I didn't. Will seemed to understand things I never allowed myself to see. That, he told me, was "the last time to see my brother whole." They grilled outside and Daddy took him to the chair he had set up looking out over the backyard. That's where Daddy made his peace with dying. Once when I was home, my mom wept and pointed out back and said, "I think he's scared and it breaks my heart."

Will said Daddy slept a lot. When he woke up, he asked his older brother to read the Bible to him. Mostly Psalms. The closest Will came to addressing what they both knew was when he read from 1 Corinthians 15, about the resurrection and how our earthly body is just temporary, and the glories of eternal life await. Neither said much about the verses. Will left that visit hopeful and at peace. The night Daddy took a turn, Mama called Uncle Will and told him he needed to hurry. Will and Becky wept during that long drive up through the Mississippi Delta toward the hospital in Memphis. They got to his bedside a half hour too late. Daddy was cold and lifeless. Uncle Will leaned over and hugged him. He kissed him and told him he loved him. Even with his faith in a coming eternal life together, Will said he had a hard time leaving his brother alone in the ground at the cemetery. He said he wanted to take him home. I felt the same way.

Since my father died, Will has worked hard to make sure that my mom, brother, and I know that he is there for us, and that he misses his brother as much as we miss our husband and father. I appreciate that about him. He makes a sustained and visible effort to be at events at which his beloved brother would have been, from family funerals on my mother's side to book events for me. He is always there, and by showing up, he has shown his love for his brother.

I love being around Will and seeing the world through his lens of childlike enthusiasm that hasn't been dimmed one bit by time. That's why, when he mentioned that he'd never been to New York City and longed to go, I told him that was a problem I could solve. So we went together, checking into a fancy SoHo hotel and spending four or five days eating bagels and pastrami from Katz's, and riding the subway, and sitting front row at *Jersey Boys*, when the old songs from his past and the memories they evoked made him cry and then stand on his toes and cheer when the cast came out to bow. We had a magical time together. My favorite night was taking him to Peter Luger with my cousin Kyser, where we ate huge steaks and had cocktails and Will told us stories about our fathers and their childhoods that we'd never known. I don't want to air family business here, but suffice it to say that it was difficult, and I understood better why the four Thompson boys were so close; their own kind of tribe. But Will's favorite thing, I believe, was when we sat at the bar at Eleven Madison Park. I saw a bottle of 23-year-old Pappy sitting on the shelf and I ordered us each a drink. I'll never forget the look on his face. I ordered us another, and we sat there, me and my father's older brother and best friend, and we sipped this beautiful, rare, expensive whiskey and we didn't need to say a thing.

- 4 -

JULIAN SPENT THE FIRST PART OF HIS LIFE not saying much. One of his father's friends called him Silent Dan. Once he got invited onto local television as a child and froze on-screen and seemed to try to fold into himself; a little boy making insecure origami out of his skinny body. That little boy has been replaced by a confident man who moves in the sophisticated world of high-end spirits, wine, and food. Julian knows his stuff. One night at dinner in Louisville at a restaurant he loves on Bardstown Road, he passed around ceviche and then nodded at this Spanish white wine he'd ordered. He wanted us to have the proper experience.

"Now take a sip of that," he said.

His older sister, Sally Van Winkle Campbell, laughed and turned to me.

"See, he was never like that," she said. "He used to be the silent type. No more!"

I considered the man I now call a friend. He wasn't always the first version of him I ever saw, dancing to Bollywood music at a late-night party. He had to learn how to be Julian Van Winkle. It's an ongoing education of a lifetime. Once he was a quiet, intense man with a mustache. That's been shaved, which is cosmetic but also symbolic. He's been reborn with his third-act success, and he has learned how to be like his grandfather, to become, through time and intention and centripetal force, the man on the bottle of whiskey he made famous. He regularly plays drums with bands. There's the story of the Kentucky Derby party when a group of famous people, including baseball star Cal Ripken, had cornered Julian to talk whiskey and Wayne Gretzky kept coming up and interrupting, until Julian finally wheeled around and said, "Why don't you shut the fuck up, *Wayne?*"

The Julian I'd seen in front of crowds seemed like an extrovert.

"Were you always a confident public speaker?" I asked him.

"I'm not confident at all," he said. "It was hard."

He trailed off.

I thought back to a conversation I had with Ed and Chenault on the *Cathedral of Bourbon* night, when all this began. Back then I didn't have the bandwidth to understand what they were telling me. There, by the band, she talked about how quiet and reserved her father was before the whiskey stuff blew up, how he'd sit quietly while Sissy ran the house. I asked Sissy about the change. She laughed and remembered the many seasons of their life and how their children saw the change happen in real time. "Like, who is this man?" she said.

His daughter Chenault told me how, now that she's grown, she understands better that he struggled to know how exactly to show the love he felt. That makes the change she's seen even more remarkable. Not long ago, her house design landed on the front of a magazine. Bursting with pride, she called her parents. Julian answered the phone. She told him and he pulled the phone away for a moment and hollered across the room, "She got the freaking cover!"

He went on and on about how proud he was of her hard work and talent, and of the business and reputation she'd built while being an amazing mother and leader in the family and that if he was the kind of man prone to tears of joy, he'd be crying them. She couldn't believe this emotional gushing. Never in her life had he ever said anything like that at all.

"Wow, Dad," she said. "Is Mom hearing all of this? I've never heard you talk like this!"

– 5 –

ONE OF THE MOST VEXING and popular quests for bourbon drinkers
is to identify who actually distilled the liquid that fills the bottles
in their home bars and collections. Four different whiskeys have
been bottled under the label of Pappy Van Winkle's Family Reserve, and that's without getting into the 10- and 12-year-old bourbon Julian sells. The first Pappy was (1) Old Boone distilled in the
1970s, because Julian was sitting on aged barrels of it that he didn't
want to go to waste. That was good whiskey. Then came a long run
of (2) Stitzel-Weller. That was great whiskey. When people think of
the Pappy taste, that's what they're imagining. Julian always wondered about rating systems because, if an inferior whiskey got the
famous 99, then why didn't the otherworldly Stitzel-Weller get a
perfect 100?

His success planted the seeds of his potential demise. That 99
came just four years after Diageo had shut down the Van Winkles'

old plant and sold off Pappy's four brands for cash. The same panic that led to that now deeply regretted fire sale also led to Julian's access to those barrels. Once his whiskey had started a revolution, the big companies and other bourbon brand owners realized what he'd done and how the public had responded, and slowly those barrels became harder and harder to find. Julian could see into the future. A day would come when nobody would sell him whiskey. He understood the problem but didn't know how to solve it without getting his family back into the distilling business. Then, in 2001, as he searched for a possible solution, a solution found him: Buffalo Trace called with the idea of a joint venture. The company offered Julian a symbolic union that appealed to his love of tradition: a rejoining of the Van Winkles with the W. L. Weller brand that Buffalo Trace had bought from Diageo two years before, along with its precious stocks of aged, wheated, Stitzel-Weller bourbon. It was perfect. Almost.

The Buffalo Trace–distilled Pappy Van Winkle's Family Reserve would not be available for fifteen years. But Julian didn't have fifteen years of Stitzel-Weller left. You see the problem.

The math didn't work. Julian Van Winkle would run out of Stitzel-Weller before he could bottle the Buffalo Trace, which is made from the same mash bill his family used back on Limestone Lane. Julian needed bourbon, and not just any bourbon. He needed to protect his reputation as the best in the world, and not get caught up in negative publicity about changing the mythic Pappy "formula," even though there really isn't a formula at all, just a complex interaction of grains and water and wood and weather and time. It's funny: when you start to learn about bourbon, you imagine it as an art, and the more you learn, the more you discover it's a science. But there comes a point when even the experts dissemble and shrug and admit they don't actually know how all those factors work together and interplay, and that's when you start to see it as art again.

The best barrels he found at the time were made by (3) Bernheim.

Now that's where it got tricky.

The Bernheim distillation wasn't his favorite—some barrels were better than others—but it still had the Van Winkle wheated mash bill. The old Stitzel-Weller bones were in place. And sometimes that shone through and he loved the whiskey. Other times he tasted some harshness and in some barrels an underlying flavor that came from the construction of the still and from the yeast that Diageo used. Whiskey, as he told me over and over again, is fragile. When Diageo shut down the Stitzel-Weller plant and replaced it with a new one, the company accidentally lost its ability to make the same consistently wonderful bourbon that had been made since Derby Day 1935. The Bernheim whiskey was good but not what his palate identified as that powerful taste of home. Using it was a risk, yes, but one he'd have to take to stay in business.

He'd rebuilt his family's reputation on Stitzel-Weller, which he loved and which many bourbon aficionados consider the finest whiskey ever made, and now he was putting all that into the hands of something that was not his favorite. Some experts didn't like it, not picking it as exceptional in blind tests. But many people loved it. And more tellingly, many people didn't even notice, as the price for Pappy kept spiraling upward on the secondary market. But I believe it made Julian feel like a little bit of a fraud. He never said this to me directly but I think he lived in fear that someone would make a big deal out of the Bernheim Pappy or he'd get asked in a public forum and have to say either that he didn't like his own highly touted whiskey or, even worse, lie and say he did. Nobody ever asked, at least not directly enough that he had to answer. Now those fifteen years have passed, and there's (4) Buffalo Trace distillation whiskey sitting on a table waiting for him.

- 6 -

THE TASTING THAT I'D DRIVEN UP FOR is the next year's 15-year-old Pappy Van Winkle's Family Reserve. That wait was finally over for him. I was anxious. Julian got to work. A stack of towels sat in the third drawer down. A plastic clipboard showed a list of all the barrels and their locations in the rickhouses. The most important people in the making of whiskey are the folks who control how and where and when the barrels are stored, from higher floors to cooler ones, using the changing temperatures and varied airflows and idiosyncratic climates of the storage facilities to impact the color, taste, and character of the liquid inside the barrels. Julian checked the information: D-6-19, I-1-18, digits as meaningful to him as they were inscrutable to me. In all there were one hundred ninety barrels. Julian took a sip and held the glass up to the light. A sign read, QUIET PLEASE, TASTERS AT WORK.

He gushed over No. 116 and No. 107 and made notes to himself.

Barrels 103 and 104 were hot, which means they hit your mouth with a fierce, alcoholic burn. When they found a barrel the tasters thought was bad, they wrote an *X* on the bottle in Sharpie. Julian and I were tasting when Kevin Nowaczyk, one of the Buffalo Trace experts, came in to join him at the tasting table.

"We've found five or six good ones," Julian said, nodding. "A little sweet, some too dry."

"There's a character, too, especially the wheated bourbons, that as things get older they kind of pick up this syrupy sweetness," Kevin said. "I don't know if you've ever smelled ether but . . . ethereal?"

Julian and I laughed.

"Oh yeah, when I was four or five years old I got my tonsils out," Julian said.

"I was in Las Vegas . . . ," I cracked.

Kevin laughed, too.

"Never go up against a man in the depths of an ether binge," he said.

We got on with the tasting. "There's just like this solvent-y sweetness," Kevin said, "not quite like acetone or gasoline but I think ether is the best description. At least that's what I pick up all the time."

"Spoken like a true chemist," Julian said.

"I actually did career day at school for my daughter the other day," Kevin said, "and I had to kind of dance around what I did and I said I'm someone who combines chemical compounds to make stuff, and my eight-year-old daughter yelled really loudly, 'He makes beer.'"

We did this for a while—drinking whiskey, to state the obvious, happens a lot when you're hanging with Julian, from really rare Stitzel-Weller white dog to old bottles of Maker's Mark—and to be honest, it gets repetitive after a while. I know, I know. But if you're reading this to get inside the making and selling of Pappy Van Winkle, I'm duty bound to report that drinking some of the best bourbon in the world can get tiresome. But that very monotony is what made this particular tasting so special. It looked like all the others. I mean, tastings are all the same—unremarkable, undramatic—until this summer. In some ways, this was the day he'd been anticipating since he packed up and left behind that falling-down rattrap bottling plant full of raining vodka and raccoon shit. It was the beginning of the rest of his life, and of Preston's life, and of the life of their family brand, which began long before Julian was born and would hopefully live on long after he dies. He was tasting a 15-year-old Pappy made of the wheated bourbon produced on-site by Buffalo Trace. Sometimes a brand is an invented thing to sell people on an idea. For Julian, seeing Pappy on each bottle is personal. It matters to him that the bourbon carries on the philosophical ideal of his family's old distillery. He's been involved in every stage of this process and now it's time to find out how they did. It had been a long wait.

- 7 -

FOR ALL THE SCIENCE THAT TAKES PLACE in the lab, and for all my mocking of the idea of magic, there is something about the landscape that finds its way into these bottles that are filled in Kentucky and then sent out around the world. The bourbon inside is a note sent by shipwrecked people to let someone out over the horizon know that they are still alive, and to maybe transmit some of the culture, too. The sunlight that shines down on the fields that bear the grains that become the whiskey leaves the sun eight minutes and twenty seconds before it warms the earth and gives life to those plants. We are always living in the past and every bottle carries that time travel with it into the world, sealed tight against the oxidizing danger of the air. Maybe whiskey is so fragile because once the cap comes off, the past rushes out of the bottle and is gone forever.

Throughout the past three years, I've spent a lot of time in Kentucky, for this book and for a television show I produce called *TrueSouth*, which featured the state in one of the episodes. So much time on the ground has forced me to really consider this place, and the idea of bourbon as a document kept growing stronger and stronger. I make the show with the writer John T. Edge and the director Tim Horgan. In it, we travel around the South and try to strip away myth and reveal the place as it is, not as people might wish in their sepia-toned memories for it to have been. For one episode, I spent a lot of time driving around bourbon country in Kentucky, and that time changed the way I saw Julian and his whiskey. I grew up in a farming community, so the emotional value of land was hardwired into me at a young age. I saw that same kind of love in Kentucky and I realized that if half of making whiskey is industrial, then the other half is agrarian. Bourbon is a crop as surely as cotton or soybeans or rice. This sentiment hit home when our television show landed in a Kentucky farming community named Hodgenville, where the eighth and ninth generations of men and women worked their family land, and in the nearby self-proclaimed Bourbon Capital of the World, Bardstown. In between them, right on the county line, was a little place called New Haven. It's a county-line town, which gives it an outlaw feel. All over the South, the Baptists and the bootleggers have long worked to keep some counties dry while others stayed wet. That meant county-line runs by teenagers in cars, looking for a six-pack or a quart—Oxford,

Mississippi, to the Panola county line—or by semitruck, hauling thousands of cases in large and complex bootlegging operations, transporting beer and liquor from a wet county to a dry one.

A couple of times on our initial scouting trip of Kentucky, we stopped at a liquor store called Mouser's in New Haven, usually at the end of a workday, to get a cold Budweiser and a pint of Barton's. We drank the beers at the counter, talking to one of the owners, who wore diamond rings on all his fingers. Old men eyed us while playing cards and throwing spent peanut shells on the floor. Mounted deer heads hung on the walls and the cardplayers joked about growing pot. If you've ever heard the song "Copperhead Road," these are the folks it's about: *DEA's got a chopper in the air. . . .* They don't like strangers in county-line towns. You can tell by the tension you feel in every room you enter, until someone gives you the blessing, and suddenly people relax.

We hung out at the counter and let this place wash over us—a deeply Catholic town, where most everyone grew up with a dozen siblings. Shrines made of Virgin Mary statues rest in the oval porcelain shade of abandoned bathtubs. Kentucky remains full of these little worlds somehow protected against the ravenous American homogeneity. The state does microcultures well. Down the road in Monroe County, there is a hyperlocal style of barbecue, rising from the daily rhythms of factory life, during which a pork shoulder is cut thin on a band saw and cooked quickly over hickory scraps from sawmills, suiting the short lunch breaks allowed the factory shifts. Hundreds of these bubbles exist.

Kentucky still feels like the frontier. It's hard to explain but palpable on the ground and especially on the road: US Route 31, Kentucky Route 63, Glasgow to Eighty-Eight to Summer Shade, rocketing with the windows down, passing farms that have been in the same family for generations. You could feel all that leaning against the counter at Mouser's, sipping on a Budweiser, listening to the stories, and clocking the diamond rings that looked like twinkling brass knuckles when the owner made a fist. During our first trip to Mouser's, we all wondered how we might get this strange hidden world on camera. It seemed vital to explaining the place, because to most local farmers, there's no difference between growing cotton and bootlegging whiskey, between fields of wheat and of bright-green funky marijuana crops growing in their shadow to hide them from those DEA flights. In Kentucky, the founding spirit of whiskey has been co-opted by businesses but that spirit didn't just go away. If you want to see the lengths a man is willing to go to protect his homeplace, whether it's turning a rotting rye crop into whiskey or planting rows of pot mixed in with his corn, then just get on the back roads and drive.

To get our television cameras inside Mouser's, we needed someone with maximum credibility. We decided on a now reformed drug kingpin from around these parts. Joe Keith Bickett was a member of the famed Cornbread Mafia, the largest domestic drug cartel ever assembled, all in the counties around Mouser's and the famous bourbon distilleries. Joe Keith did his twenty-plus years, was released, and now works for a law firm. He also wrote two hilarious books about his experiences. So Joe Keith walked into Mouser's and found one of the owners at the counter. "Tell us about back in the bootlegging days," he asked. "Come on, man, about how it was back in the sixties?"

"It used to be we were the only liquor store till you got to Murfreesboro, Tennessee," the owner told him. "We had a bootleg business. We probably have had more beer go out the back of this store than we did go out the front. And my uncle worked here and my daddy . . . and all they did was haul booze. But then, as the years went through, Hardin County went wet, Warren County went wet, now you got Pulaski County wet. You got Clinton County wet. You got Cumberland County wet. You got Edmonson County wet. You've got Taylor County wet. You've got all these counties . . ."

The voters of LaRue County just passed their alcohol law by ten votes, pushed by politicians who wanted to figure out how to catch some money from the bourbon boom that's bringing wealth into so many counties around them. To most farmers, there's not much difference between moonshining and bootlegging, between growing pot and supplying corn to big distilleries; this is farming country and all a farmer wants is to make enough money from his land to be able to pass it on to the next generation. Bourbon, when made from local crops, is a physical manifestation of deeply American ideas about home and land and independence. As Joe Keith said when asked about his route to being a drug kingpin, "We didn't see where that would be any harder to grow than soybeans."

In the end, more than seventy people were arrested and charged for being part of the Cornbread Mafia. Some of them remain in jail. A few won't ever get out. Zero of the convicted men testified against their friends or enemies. Nobody rolled. Not one person. There are actual mafia members who have snitched at the drop of a subpoena, but these Kentucky farmboys did their time and kept their mouths shut. That's the best description of what it feels like to sit at Mouser's and drink a beer as a card game goes on behind you, or to drive these winding Kentucky roads past meth trailers or horse farms, whether getting a half-pint in a bootlegger's shack of a store or driving a manicured road that winds down to a distillery where Julian Van Winkle is sitting at a lazy Susan, tasting dozens of barrels of whiskey, trying to remember how Stitzel-Weller tasted when he was a much younger man.

I feel like Pappy is with Julian as he sits down to taste, not the legend but the man himself, Julian's grandfather, who hunted and golfed with a dog named Thunder. If you dig back into the past, flip through old newspapers in the small Kentucky town where he grew up, you'll find Pappy's own history: a successful attorney, a father, a brother who owned his own empire of coal mines and led an effort to have a hydroelectric dam and electric plant built; a modern man looking to the future. But go one more generation back, to Pappy's own grandfather, a man named Miciah Van Winkle who moved to Kentucky, to the very edge of civilization, where he sought and ultimately made a prosperous new life, enough to launch his sons and grandsons into the business world and the heights of Kentucky society. And he did it like so many first-generation dreamers: he was a farmer. That's the life Pappy wanted to re-create, the life he did re-create at the Stitzel-Weller distillery he opened on Derby Day because, as his brother looked to the future and its new sources of energy and power, Pappy spent his life looking backward and selling the nostalgia he felt to other men who felt it, too.

- 8 -

LONGING FOR A VANISHED AGRARIAN PAST (that possibly never existed) dominates much of the American story. It's human nature. I
recently watched that Ken Burns *Country Music* documentary and
wasn't surprised to learn that the genre was invented and popular-
ized by urban people who'd left an agrarian life behind. They were
nostalgic for a world that had been lost. Baseball has the same
roots, as do the meat-and-three country cooking places all over the
South. Soul food and country cooking, the black and white expres-
sions of the same traditions, emerged in cities when people left the
farms and tried to live a new kind of life, working in factories and
longing for the way they remembered the past, which often has
little in common with the actual past they lived. Bourbon carries
all those ideas, too. American whiskey was something farmers made
when they lived too far from market to sell their grains. A bottle of
bourbon with a tax sticker in a store is the creation of corporate

America, often bought by people who instinctively know that if they believe the lie, then they can reclaim some of the country where those farmers once lived and plowed before mostly vanishing from the earth. Trying to hold on to that spirit drives our politics and culture and even works in our individual lives.

I grew up working on the sprawling cotton farm owned by Cliff Heaton, a hard job in the Mississippi heat, and I've gotten a lot of self-mythologizing mileage out of those hours in the sun. I get to say I grew up working on a farm, and that's true as a biographical detail. Early in the morning, before six a.m., I'd get up and make my way to the gin to find out where we'd be working that day. Then a long line of us would park on a turnrow and get in the fields, carrying a long-handled hoe, moving up one row and back down another, looking for and eliminating weeds. I love to tell the stories. They reinforce my own self-image as a grinder and someone who outworked other people to get my job, but I often leave out other biographical details that might tell a different kind of story: I grew up the son of a trial lawyer and my mother's family owns nearly ten thousand acres of prime Mississippi Delta farmland, some of the most fertile and valuable agricultural dirt in the world.

Both my mother and father grew up in farming families, and both those farms were in places that became known for the blues musicians who lived, worked, suffered, and played there. If whiskey comes from the land itself, then the blues is its close cousin, at least in the way that I thought about them. My dad grew up in Bentonia, Mississippi, which has its own eponymous style of music, made famous by Skip James. The epicenter of this world was a juke joint named the Blue Front Cafe. Growing up, my dad and his brothers could hear that music from their bedroom but weren't allowed to go in. There was a white world and a black world. One summer, one of my uncles got recording equipment and did his own version of Alan Lomax and recorded some old bluesmen, some of whom worked on my grandfather's farm. When Granddaddy found the reels and heard the black music on them, he took them all and burned them. I believe a lot of things died in that pile of melting tape.

We had a family funeral out on my dad's land not long ago. My cousin Miller, a sweet young man, died of an accidental drug overdose. He was my uncle Will's first grandchild and Will adored him. Even now, he weeps listening to Miller's favorite songs on a CD his daughter made him, and when the last track "I'll Fly Away" comes on, he is brought low and cannot listen any longer.

Music is often the kingdom the dead inhabit in our souls. The bluesman Jimmy "Duck" Holmes, a friend of the family, came out to pay his respects and brought another young bluesman with him to play some songs: Blues for Miller. I felt a lot in that music and in Mr. Holmes's presence at our terribly sad gathering, which conveyed a bit of hope that we were all human beings, all Mississippians, and that if we correctly remember our past and the roles all our ancestors played in it—both mine and Mr. Holmes's—then we have a chance to get it right. Being Southern means carrying a responsibility to shake off the comforting blanket of myth and see ourselves clearly. I was bringing a child into this world, and into our long history of trying to do the right thing while benefitting mightily from the wrong thing, and I wanted her to love our home and our family, but to see it clearly and without the nostalgia that so often softens my anger and desire to tear it all down and build a new world in its place.

Not long after the funeral for Miller, my uncles Will and Michael sold the farm and the cabin. I didn't want to sell but so much of the responsibility for upkeep landed on Uncle Will that I didn't have the standing or right to disagree. Deep inside, I believe that losing Miller left Will with too many painful memories when he visited the place, as if some sacred idea that lived there had died with him. Before we turned it over to the new owners, I asked for a favor. My dad and his brothers had built the cabin on the lake themselves and then written their names in the concrete foundation. Will understood my request and I feel like it pleased him. He got someone with a big saw to cut out the rectangle where my dad had signed his name and added the date: June 20, 1967. That was a Tuesday. One of the hottest songs was "A Whiter Shade of Pale." Muhammad Ali got sentenced to five years for refusing to fight in Vietnam. Three days before, Secretary of Defense Robert McNamara had commissioned the top-secret report that would show that the government knew Vietnam could not be won and sent young boys my dad's age to die anyway. My dad joined ROTC in college and was headed to Southeast Asia when the US Army offered to let him trade his fifteen months' active duty for a long stretch in the reserves. He jumped at the chance and instead of dying in a war the generals already knew was lost, he moved to Clarksdale, Mississippi, to start a career and a family. Five years later, I was born.

I just now stood up from writing and went outside and rubbed my hand over my dad's signature, trying to feel close to him. The script is fading, a prayer to four brothers and the dreams their children now try to realize for them, as ours will do one day, too. That piece of the old porch is a treasure to me. When a house I am planning in Montana is finally built, I am going to drive the concrete north and make sure a piece of my family lives in this new home. Seeing it just now left me feeling empty and sad and protective. It's the only tangible thing I have left of a once sprawling way of life. For perhaps the first time, I think I really understand how Julian feels about his memories of Stitzel-Weller that drive him when he sits down to choose the whiskey that will go into a bottle of Pappy.

- 9 -

MY MOTHER GREW UP IN SHELBY, Mississippi, daughter of a land-owner who farmed many more acres than my dad's family. Her family bought the land in 1927, and by the time my uncle took over in 1968, the farm had shrunk to seventeen hundred acres. My uncle, Rives, has spent five decades in his quest to return it to its original size. That farm is his life's work. Rives is the most remarkable man I know, a human being of great empathy and courage—a staunch liberal in a state and profession where he is often the only person in the room with his views. He's a financial wizard who has chosen as his craft the re-creation of our farm. He's been successful in his foolish and beautiful goal, one that will take care of my children and my children's children, long after all of us are gone. I've grown to love it more with time, as things like roots mean more to me. The farm sits along the right side of the road, headed south, between Clarksdale and Cleveland, Mississippi. That's smack in the Mississippi Delta, where the famous Delta blues were born. The famous bluesman Big Jack Johnson worked for my uncle on the farm. My dad was his lawyer. When I hear the Delta blues, I feel like my father must have felt whenever he heard Skip James. That music was the soundtrack of the juke joints I went to in high school, places like Miss Sarah's in downtown Clarksdale, or that bar out across Highway 61, past Lyon, and even now that music transports me to a specific place and time. On my last trip to Clarksdale, I went to Red's near the Sunflower River bridge, one of the last operating juke joints, and the singer went around the packed room asking people where they were from. Soon enough, he asked me.

"Eight blocks that way," I said, pointing.

He smiled. I think he smiled. "The other side of the tracks," he said.

He wasn't wrong. There are railroad tracks separating the two halves of Clarksdale. I nodded and when he finished, I realized I was the only person in the room from Clarksdale. Everyone else was a tourist, and it hit me that I, too, was a kind of tourist to the blues: I am from *around* the world that created that music, but I can never be from *inside* it. I am from the Mississippi Delta but not from the land of the Delta blues. That hit me hard. Wallace will inherit this world, and I mean literally. She will be a landowner in this place and I want her to understand what that means. There are two Clarksdales, two Deltas, two different ways to hear the blues. While I was making an episode of my television show in Memphis, focusing on the rural-urban interplay in a city so close to the suffering of the Delta, a woman talked about how her father carried the memory of Clarksdale and Coahoma County cotton fields with him long after he put down his hoe and moved to the city. She remembers him saying one night to her mother, his wife, "You don't know what it's like to work on a plantation."

He didn't mean just walking rows in the sun. I've done that. He meant the dawning hopelessness. The realization that there would only ever be another row. In that sense, no matter what I like to say or believe, I never worked on a farm, because I always knew it was a way station on the way to someplace brighter. I never once felt hopeless. So I never worked on a plantation, no matter how many hours I spent on one. This all makes me think a lot about what it means to be from the Mississippi Delta; to be from the South. For me and other white people of a certain social class, it means that I carry a legacy of a roguish and faded gentility, a love for whiskey and fast cars on winding roads, and a knowledge of roadside blues clubs that offered guitars and tall boys of beer. To the father of the woman we interviewed, and in the shorthand of one black Mississippian talking to another, or for two people in Chicago comparing family trees, being from Clarksdale means something different entirely. There's a Muddy Waters quote in Robert Gordon's essential biography that I can't shake, because Waters is the most famous son of Clarksdale, and he has become a patron saint of the blues tourism that is at the center of my hometown's attempt to survive. Muddy, the quote implied, would be fine if it didn't survive at all, if it all died and turned to dust and blew away with that nutrient-rich topsoil that kept so many of his kin buried in the South. "I wanted to get out of Mississippi in the worst way," he said. "Go back? What I want to go back for?"

These dual and contradictory views of the same place define virtually every story told about this part of the world, including the story about whiskey. Especially the story of whiskey. Kentucky brands itself clearly and proudly as Southern, home of fried chicken and brown liquor. A lot of people don't know that Kentucky wasn't part of the Confederacy. It never seceded and yet now clearly defines itself as the South. Why would a state pretend it lost a war it actually won? More than one hundred thousand Kentuckians fought as Americans while only thirty thousand fought as Confederates. After the war, the winners went on with their lives while the losers, and later their children and then grandchildren, fought hard to redeem the people and the world lost in defeat. A historian we interviewed for our Kentucky episode of *TrueSouth* named Charles Reagan Wilson told us that the losers of the Civil War had to make sense of having been defeated in what their leaders called a "holy war," and he said something that resonated with me: "Winston Churchill said that the Irish remember the defeats long after the English have forgotten the victories. And in a sense, that was true of the Union sympathizers in Kentucky. They went on to other things. But the people who lost, their cause became the Lost Cause. And so, they're the ones, the white Kentucky Confederate sympathizers, after the war, who decide they've got to put the Confederate stamp on Kentucky for the future. . . . The ministers had told them they were fighting a holy war. How do you lose a holy war? The typical wording on a Confederate monument in Kentucky, and in other places, was, LEST YE FORGET. It's on almost all of them."

It's important to know our past, all of it, the beautiful and the ugly, and it is also important to value our families and carry their memories with us, which often creates the urge to polish and clean and erase. Those competing needs—to look clearly at our home while also sculpting our past into a carrying case for familial identity—are at the heart of nearly every part of Southern life. When I tell my daughter, Wallace, the story of the place she's from—when I play Muddy Waters or Son House or Skip James—I want her to see the complete picture. I want her to hear that music and know that people like us—planters and landowners, which we are—often caused the pain these musicians turned into beauty. Let the sound flooding out of her speakers carry both histories: the memory of when she first heard that beautiful music living side by side with the knowledge of what trauma summoned it from the earth. If both can exist to her at the same time, then we just might find a way to keep walking toward the light.

~ 10 ~

JULIAN BECAME SOMEONE I KNEW I'D CONSULT if I ever had to make a big decision. I trusted him, and so one evening sitting at my kitchen island, with a question really working away inside, I impulsively pulled out my phone and sent him a message. *Do you believe in God?* The next day, he gave me his answer in the form of a few stories, which is the way Julian often makes a point he cares about.

On March 13, 1979, Sissy gave birth to three identical girls who were born perfectly healthy. They'd read all the literature about how the odds of complications go up with two babies and go up again with triplets. Julian thought they were incredibly lucky, and that there was the hand of the Almighty at work. That could be luck, though. So he told another story.

They've got friends who also go to Michigan in the summer. Years ago their small child found his way out of a window onto the second-floor roof. Below, a grouping of round lake rocks anchored a landscaping feature. The boy fell off the roof and hurtled toward the ground, and his head just missed all those rocks and he landed soft and unhurt. His mother had a sister die at a very young age and so she and her family and friends, including Julian and Sissy, believed that an angel had been watching over them all these years and, on that day, made sure the boy found his way down to the one place where he might live. But that could just be coincidence, as could all the times Julian did something stupid and should have died, like when he rolled that car with Frances, but those could be luck. But Julian knows that faith is always the belief in the unseen, and the unseeable, and so he believes that there are forces at work somewhere beyond the curtain. I want to believe my daddy sees me live my life and is around, just out of my vision, and that I will watch over Wallace one day.

I want to have Julian's faith. He believes Pappy and his father know the road he's walked. He believes we are watched over. That we all have angels. Two close friends of his, a father and a son, died several years ago in a hunting-lodge fire—Edward Chesley Greene Sr. and Edward Chesley Greene Jr. of Mobile, Alabama. Julian keeps their picture in his wallet, with a prayer attached to it. Yes, he told me, there is a God. I don't know what I think but it does make me stop and consider, knowing that every time I've ever been with him, he's carried a prayer in his wallet, a talisman to summon guardian angels, and he's never mentioned it to me.

- 11 -

I'VE BEEN LOOKING FOR THE SAME KIND OF ROOTS. Lately I've felt a bit lost, waiting on my daughter to be born, wondering if I am up to the task in front of me. I've been reading Thomas Merton. His writings offer the best path I can find for my own return to the church—or to God, really, since I believe I'm done with church—and I find comfort and peace in his worldview. I want to believe in something larger than us, and the closest I come is when I'm reading Merton. There's a sign in Louisville marking the spot where he had a vision of how humans on this rock of ours should live together. He later wrote: *In Louisville, at the corner of Fourth and Walnut, in the center of the shopping district, I was suddenly overwhelmed with the realization that I loved all those people, that they were mine and I theirs, that we could not be alien to one another even though we were total strangers.*

Writing about bourbon meant a few visits to the Maker's Mark distillery in rural Kentucky, and I discovered that Merton lived and wrote at a monastery that is a thirteen-mile straight shot down Highway 52 from Maker's Mark. There's a honky-tonk in between that has a mural of Hank Williams painted on the front, so the Hillbilly Shakespeare can watch over the people who come inside for escape. I got to know that road well. One afternoon I left the distillery with John T. Edge. We passed shiny new farms with gleaming grain silos and abandoned farms with weathered and collapsed barns. People rising. People falling.

I missed the turn into the monastery, and as I wheeled around, we saw a simple homemade sign.

TO THE STATUES, it read.

Neither of us knew what that meant, so we got out of the car and walked into the woods. Every so often, there'd be another sign.

TO THE STATUES.

We crossed a simple footbridge and looked down into deep gulches and hollers. We crossed a dam across a peaceful lake in which a man dressed in white silently fished. We climbed a simple ladder into the foothills and kept winding, passing little shrines and religious statues along the way. John T. and I both felt what I can only call a mystical twinge. I felt like I'd driven out here to bucket list–check a gravestone—a celebration of a great man's death—and instead stumbled into a celebration of how he lived. We joked that maybe there were no statues, that *we* were the statues, or perhaps our worldly cares and anxieties and vanities, and that we were looking for some sort of cosmic mirror out here in the woods. A single cardinal sat on a limb and looked at us. We heard rain hitting the canopy high above but no water touched our faces. The high-pitched whine of tires on the highway down below grew more and more faint. The farther we walked, the more I started to really notice the plants and the little benches offering beautiful hillside views. I didn't want the walk to end, and I *always* want a walk to end.

I've been ordering my life foolishly. A voice of warning has been growing louder as I considered what being a father actually means. When I make an accounting of myself honestly, I do not like what I find. Always a pleaser, I have put satisfying bosses above myself or the needs of my family and friends. I have put worldly success at the top of my hierarchy of needs and lived accordingly, hoping that the people who loved me would love me enough to indulge and forgive. Even this walk felt illicit. It had been an embarrassingly long time since I just did something unplanned in the middle of a workday. Normally we are grinding.

I think about my wife as we walk, about what she's doing now. Sonia is so important to every part of my life that her presence often exists as a shadow in everything I do. The happiest I ever am is when she smiles. When she's happy, it makes me happy, and when she's not, I spiral with her. We are connected in that way. Marriage is a strange thing. I love my wife. She bet on me at a time when maybe that didn't seem like the best option. Her relentless desire to do things well runs through every corner of her life and now mine. I love to make her laugh. She makes me laugh all the time—her timing is professional. If you are her friend, she is there for you no matter what. I love that about her. I feel unworthy of her. My work often feels like something I choose instead of her, and I worry about how patient she is about that.

In the last years of his life, Alabama football coach Bear Bryant read a devotional over and over again, a window into how he appraised his successful and famous life; his own sorting out of the things he gained and what it cost him. "When tomorrow comes," it read, "this day will be gone forever, leaving something in its place I have traded for it." I feel like I am forever making bad trades. I wonder if I'm just repeating the mistakes of my father. My parents talked a lot about going to China to see those gorges. My father died and they never made the trip. Now the gorges have been destroyed by a hydroelectric dam that powers televisions and washing machines and personal laptop computers. The future is waiting, and it is never the vision the hopeful word conjures, so I want my love for my wife and child to eclipse whatever love I have for my work (which is just another way of saying "for myself"). I worry I won't be worthy of this child, or of my wife, and that I won't be able to find the version of myself who is called upon to stand up in this new act of life and be a man.

We walked for nearly a mile, moving through clearings and along narrow winding paths with nature close in on our shoulders. We talked about the idea that all of our human vanities—obsessing about bourbon, or writing about sports or food, or anything really—are just our attempts to fill a God-size hole in our lives. I felt closer to God, or to some higher power, than I had in a very long time.

Then we found the statues.

We saw Jesus, his face covered in agony, and Mary weeping, and we read the dedication to Father Jonathan Daniels, an Episcopal priest killed in the heat of the civil rights movement by a shotgun-carrying sheriff's deputy, putting his body in front of a seventeen-year-old. As the cop pulled the trigger, Father Daniels pushed the young girl out of the way and threw himself into the line of fire. He took that full load of the 12-gauge and bled out. The man who killed him was acquitted and died an old man. Like the coward he was, the sheriff's deputy claimed self-defense for killing an un-armed priest. It took me ten seconds to find the killer's son's Face-book page, where he wishes Trump a happy birthday and posts from a dubious news site about how anti-Kavanaugh protesters were paid to be there. There's clearly no attempt to erase the stain of sin from his family, only to replace facts with myth, to protect a past unworthy of protection. I have shameful ghosts in my family, too, like an uncle who ran a powerful white supremacist organiza-tion in Mississippi during the civil rights movement, and I want to make sure Wallace sees them and knows that there is another way. She will inherit the power to make our family into whatever she wants it to be. After standing around and then walking alone in the woods some more, I knew we had to rejoin our day.

We walked back down to the car.

A fish jumped in the lake. The fisherman in white silently watched for ripples.

- 12 -

JULIAN LOOKED AT THE BOTTLES of 15-year-old raw Pappy in front of him.

To the side, he had a bottle of last year's Pappy 15 release.

Normally, that control bottle served as a kind of cheat sheet to compare flavor profiles. But this year, that bottle was completely useless. This was about as real as you could ever see the whiskey business. When the bourbon came out next year, it would have the exact same label and price tag as it did the year before. But it wouldn't be the same. Julian sat at the lazy Susan and I tried to imagine what he must be thinking. For fifteen years, ever since he agreed to bring his label into this huge liquor conglomerate, he'd known that one day he'd be proven right or wrong. Yes, the joint venture gave him a limitless future and a constant supply of whiskey. But would the whiskey be good? Would he like it? All those years ago he'd tasted young whiskey and wheated white dog and used his palate to make a judgment call. Was he right?

He wasn't thinking any of that because he was here doing work. The world's greatest fly rod maker once told me something that stuck: zen is a butt in a seat. That's what craft really is. Doing something over and over again without cheating or cutting corners. Julian pointed at the bottle of last year's Pappy.

"This is Bernheim whiskey," he said.

That was the past.

Then Julian turned back to the half-pints and to the future. He should have said, "This is Buffalo Trace," because that's the distillery that made the bourbon now in the half-pint in front of him for tasting. But because Freud is a motherfucker—Julian had meant to say one thing, but something else had accidentally come out—he'd revealed inadvertently what he *really* thought and felt.

"This is Stitzel-Weller," he said.

He is the last of something. The bridge, in the bourbon world and in his family, that can connect the mythology of those old whiskeys with the reality of the new ones. Someday very soon there won't be a drop of Stitzel-Weller left. If there was a barrel somewhere that's been poured into a stainless-steel tank to stop the aging, it will end up being used. Those old bottles will be opened and poured. When all that happens, Stitzel-Weller will only exist within Julian's ability to remember—and in his attempts to curate and sell something that's as close to it as his memory can get. That's what Julian brings to the tasting room alongside Kevin's science background: his memory. The more time I spent in Kentucky and on thinking about the South where I grew up and where I live, the more two related themes emerged over and over again: the power and the fragility of memory. Bourbon embodies both. It can carry the past far into the future, so that Julian can drink whiskey his grandfather and father had made, and yet he can watch that whiskey start to go bad the moment he pulls the cork until it is ruined within a few hours.

They are all betting that the bourbon boom will continue. It's a funny game. Once, the great distillers struggled because they had too much bourbon, and now they struggle because they don't have enough. This is an industry that requires peering into the future and determining which America will exist in a decade—for Julian, it requires twice that—and that's a nearly impossible thing to do. We're asking people to predict a national mood; to predict our fears and hopes. It's nearly impossible to guess what consumers will need in ten years or fifteen or twenty or twenty-three. Bourbon booms are tied mostly to a sense of nostalgia and longing—to memory— and when the brown stuff is flying off the shelves, you can bet that we are unsure of where we are going and in need of a vehicle to take us back. Vodka is for the skinny and scotch is for the strivers and bourbon is for the homesick. So sitting with Julian in the tasting room was seeing a man looking for a way back home, standing on one side of a river and needing to get across. He was trying to remember a taste from his past, and to find some modern version of it close enough to bridge that gap in his mind, between Great Buffalo Trace and Limestone Lane. He felt gratitude for Harlen Wheatley, the master distiller who'd overseen the birth of this whiskey.

Julian sipped the 15-year-old Pappy. He looked at the label to see when it was distilled: April 22, 2002. Two days before, I'd been in my first job, sitting in Rayne, Louisiana, outside Breaux Bridge, waiting with LSU wide receiver Josh Reed for him to be picked in the NFL Draft. Everyone had expected him to go in the first round, enough that his town had thrown him a party and the mayor had invited me to attend. Then hours passed and he didn't get picked, and I wanted to be as far away as I could. That was a lifetime ago for me. Josh Reed would have a long career in the NFL, by the way.

Julian tried to remember what he was doing in April of 2002. The dates on these bottles all meant something to him. They are the story of his life and his past. Then it hit him. Of course.

On April 22, 2002, Julian was negotiating with the parent company of Buffalo Trace, deciding on the right path for his label and for the legacy of his family, and less than two months later, those negotiations led to a deal, and he signed, and he carried his tradition and palate and hopes with him away from the obscurity of Lawrenceburg and toward the bright lights of Buffalo Trace and the cult whiskey road he now knows as his own.

- 13 -

THERE WAS NO DRAMATIC BUILDUP or single moment of revelation once he started tasting. He was a working man and this was work. But after just a few samples, we both agreed that this bourbon was fantastic, and that he liked it, liked it a lot, which made for a happy, relieved Julian. I held a glass in my hand, lost in my own world where I got to just sit and drink 15-year-old Van Winkle and call it work, and when I looked over at him he nodded. Julian was a stoic man, but I knew him well enough to know when he was pleased. He was pleased. I liked that he was pleased.

"I'm glad you're here to test this," he said. "It will come out in the fall."

Finding that the bourbon made at Buffalo Trace was not only good to the experts but also good to him filled him with joy—and, I think, relief. Julian had been under a cloud of anxiety that lifted immediately when he tasted these bourbons and not only liked them but loved them, and he even got taken on a memory trip when they hit his tongue. Bourbon either makes the trip or it doesn't. A son either makes the trip or he doesn't. A family tradition, whether it's whiskey or simply a big Thanksgiving dinner, either makes the trip or it doesn't.

There are endless variables that can derail, but only intention and a healthy dose of timing and luck can keep a train on the track. Julian knows he's lucky. He knows he's worked hard and endured but he also knows he's lucky. He's lucky to have found the barrels of Stitzel-Weller, and lucky to have beaten cancer, and lucky to have a family that nurtured this life out of the dirt. He remembers the hunting dogs next to the cooper shop, and Thunder hauling his granddaddy's clubs, and the smell of that whiskey bath in the summer of 1968, and the taste that entered through every pore and remained lodged in his memory long after he'd washed that whiskey away. Julian fell in love that day and is still in love. All he wants when he drinks a glass of whiskey, or when he sells you a bottle of whiskey, is for that feeling to come alive again. For him, it only comes when he tastes Stitzel-Weller, although he knows everyone has their own personal triggers; the tastes and smells that are unique to them and their own history. What he offers to his customers, though, is the trigger to *his* memories. It's an intimate transaction if you look at it right. "This is back the way that it used to be," he said with a glow, "and if you compare this to Stitzel-Weller, it's close."

- 14 -

ALL WE CAN ASK FOR IS FOR REAL LIFE to get close to the impossible myths and nostalgias that drive and seduce in equal measure. Close is a miracle. Close means that Julian had to keep his business alive in Lawrenceburg and count on Jimmy Russell and so many other angels for help, and that he had to bet on Stitzel-Weller and then sign a deal with Buffalo Trace, and then he had to wait on time to prove him right or wrong. He's been proven right. That's nearly the end of our story, although the Van Winkle family's journey is just beginning. Julian is thinking hard about a plan of succession. His daughters run a highly successful spin-off business, selling everything from needlepoint belts to barrel-aged maple syrup, everything emblazoned with the name Pappy & Company. Louise, Chenault, and Julian worked closely while renovating together a (now) beautiful building in Louisville that houses their business, and that time with his daughters made all the work and money worth it. His girls are dynamos and one day might generate more income for the family than the whiskey itself.

There's a lot to sort out, for and with the next generation, about understanding how the lifestyle piece fits with the bourbon. Combining business and family is never easy, as his father learned. Some of the estate-planning meetings turned into therapy sessions, complete with tears. Julian wakes up in the middle of the night worried if his children will all get along running the family business when he's gone. The future is out there, creeping, becoming more and more present with each passing day. He's moving on to a new phase now. His twenty years in Lawrenceburg and his fifteen years with Buffalo Trace have put the Van Winkles back atop the whiskey world. His grandfather's belief in wheat as a secondary grain and his desire to make the best bourbon from a native-born Kentucky crop instead of a holdover from Pennsylvania farmers have survived and emerged as victorious. Old Fitzgerald and its wheated descendants, from Maker's Mark to Pappy Van Winkle, are the closest human beings have yet come to bottling the ethos of Kentucky.

For Julian, making a wheated bourbon the most sought after in the world is more of a monument to his family than those two marble stones out in the shade of Louisville's Cave Hill Cemetery. He has held the line, and his son, Preston, will hold it after him, and the bourbon going out in their bottles, behind a label bearing Pappy's face, will carry Pappy's integrity, too. A few simple questions occurred to me to ask Julian: Even though you aren't sentimental, do you ever visit your father's or grandfather's graves, and do you think they'd be proud of what you've created?

He was as introspective as I'd ever seen him.

> I had to think about this one. You're pretty correct on the sentimental part!
>
> To be honest with you, I was so relieved to be out of that shithole in the holler in Lawrenceburg that almost killed me that I didn't really think about whether Pappy and Dad would be proud of me. Just glad to not anymore be dealing with so many other things there; maintenance that had nothing to do with the whiskey business. That place did serve its purpose, though, keeping me in business and that's where the "Pappy" label was created and the springboard to a better life. But it sure was nice to finally get a paycheck every now and then.
>
> I'm not much on graveyards so made no visits to Cave Hill Cemetery where they are all buried. I probably did ask my dad for help from that other dimension several times during my struggle to stay in business in the dark years.
>
> Once things got rolling with BT, and the cult whiskey thing started a few years after I joined up with them, I often thought, and tell people this constantly, that I wish Pappy and Dad were around to see what has happened to their idea of making and selling premium, aged, wheated

bourbon whiskey. Unfortunately, they were forty to sixty years too early.

Sure, they would be proud of me.

I didn't know Pappy that well but sister Sally says she sees a lot of Pappy in me.

How's that?

- 15 -

THE NEXT DAY JULIAN AND PRESTON worked around the table, finishing the tasting that started the day before. The mood was joyous. Julian loves to do this with his son. He often tells people that Preston has a better palate than he does. Preston combines his modern sensibilities with his inherited Limestone Lane vision quest. Pappy will keep evolving, which is as it should be, the whiskey a living crop borne of man living in concert with the dirt around him, and not a widget to be reproduced the same way forever.

They got to work.

Barrel 164 was empty, the clipboard said. Either it leaked or it all evaporated. That happens. You put whiskey into hibernation and pay taxes and then it's simply all gone. These are good reminders that this is much closer to farming than making steel, no matter how scientific the lab or industrial the plant.

They both loved barrels 167, 174, 175, and 176. All of them

came from the "I" rickhouse. Julian had been gushing to Preston about barrels 107 and 116, which we tasted yesterday, with Julian calling them among the best he's ever tasted, all the way back to the Stitzel-Weller Pappy. They were from the I rickhouse, too.

"First Floor I," Julian said.

"I don't know if it's a first-floor thing or an 'I' thing," Preston said.

We finished and kept talking about those two barrels.

"One hundred seven and one hundred sixteen," Julian told Preston.

"Are they gone?" Preston asked, pointing at the small bottles.

"No, they're in there," Julian said as Preston went hunting.

Julian wanted to pull his favorite and have it bottled just for him, the first single-barrel Pappy he'll ever have pulled just for the family in forty years plus. He picked barrel 107. That's a nearly perfect whiskey. The proof was 141.2, which was really high. For the first part of its life the barrel lived on the sixth floor of the C warehouse. Three or four years later, after a new hoist had been installed, the barrel was moved to the sixth floor of the D warehouse. Being on a high floor is what makes the proof so high. A lot had evaporated, with only seven cases instead of the expected twelve. The barrel moved a final time during its aging life, down to the first floor of the I warehouse, with the idea that the lower, cooler floor might let it finish its trip in a more graceful way.

A few months later, Julian invited me to Louisville to pick something up. That barrel had been bottled—a one-time only, never-to-be-repeated special edition of Pappy. Calling it an essential part of my reporting, I convinced Julian to give me some. I got in the car and headed north once again. Sonia, now seven months pregnant with our daughter, rode with me. We've always loved a road trip. The combination of the freedom of a highway and the tight confines of a car always made us our most relaxed and happy. I remember after the last election, when we both feared that the worst of the American instinct had triumphed over the best, we drove up to Montana, just to pass through the open plains and on to switchback mountain roads. We shopped at a famous tack store in Wyoming. We visited Little Bighorn and walked through the last stand of Custer. We stayed for a night in a Montana railroad town. We explored the Badlands. We kept moving, day after day, and when it ended, we felt better. Both of us took home a feeling of hope—that the majesty of America might survive the trolls who, in fear and anger, sought to shrink it.

I told Sonia a little about the past few years as I retraced the roads that had taken me to my meetings with Julian so many times before. The whiskey was a goodbye of sorts. Julian and I both understood that, I think. I loaded the whiskey into my trunk and then we went into town for dinner that night at their house. Carrie, one of the triplets, came and we all ate burgers. Sissy opened some red wine. Grandkids pinged around the house. They call Sissy "Diddy" and Julian "JuJu."

"That was my dad's nickname, too," Julian said.

Afterward Julian poured glasses of Redbreast 12. He loves Irish whiskey after a meal. That's another Van Winkle tradition. We talked about the Pappy & Company business that Carrie and Louise run. Chenault's interior design firm was booming, too, with major press and a waiting list of clients. We finished and said our good nights, leaving behind the warm glow of Julian and Sissy's home, still echoing with the energy of three generations in the same room. A beautiful feeling followed us back to our hotel. The next morning, we drove back home. The whiskey was in the trunk. I knew what I wanted to do with it. The bottles were very rare and valuable and I was going to give them to people who I knew would love and appreciate them. That's what I learned in my years with the Van Winkle family: sharing this whiskey is intrinsically tied to the spirit with which the whiskey is selected and sold. Julian hates the hoarding of it, the price gouging of it, and not just because people blame him but because that's not what bourbon was ever about anyway.

I took a bottle over to John T. Edge's house the night our television show premiered, and we sat and drank it together, and gave a little to his high school senior son, and the rest sits on his bar, waiting for another time when we'll be together.

I invited my friend Mac Nichols over to my house and made him a Vanhattan with Julian's recipe, using the 15-year-old and the rye. Mac clocked the bottle and saw the sediment and knew it hadn't been chill filtered and was therefore something strange and special. I gave him some to taste straight before mixing it into the drink and, with his sophisticated whiskey palate, he described the "crazy-thick, rich color of dark amber . . . sweet and powerful on the nose with a beautiful muted floral and rich grain aroma and all you feel is the perfect combination of vanilla, dark caramel, spice, wheat, and magic." Before he left, I smiled and handed him a bottle to take home. He was speechless and tried not to accept. I made him. Mac understands how whiskey and wine are meant to be enjoyed. When he and his wife christened their first child, he found a bottle of 1985 Krug champagne—the year he and Joli met when they were five years old in rural Mississippi—and he's saving the bottle of Pappy I gave him to open when their second child is christened. That's what whiskey is really about, especially Julian's whiskey. I thought about my uncle Will—which is just another way of thinking about family, about our past, and my father, and the promises we make to each other. One more bottle remained for me to give away. I knew what I needed to do.

- 16 -

I PACKED MY BAG for the hospital weeks before Wallace Wright Thompson was born. In it, I made sure to put one of my father's old shirts, a black-and-white checked button-down that I can still picture him wearing, and a Phi Delta Theta dad's weekend hat that I gave him in college and that he treasured. That's what I'd be wearing when I held my daughter for the first time, as a way of making sure my father was in the room. I wanted him to be a part of it. Then I got the bottle of 15-year-old Pappy out of my liquor cabinet and tucked it into the bag, too. I wanted this final handoff to be symbolic. I've learned a lot from the Van Winkles. My time with them made me examine my own life and think about my family's past and about what I want to bury and what I want to live on in my daughter. We must be intentional with our myths and stories, and we must live the lives we want our children to live.

The morning Sonia went into labor, I called our immediate

families, and then I let my uncle Will know. He and my aunt Becky got in the car in Yazoo City and rushed up to Oxford to the hospital. He texted me when they arrived. I was busy with the nurses. My mom texted me a picture of Will standing at the locked door separating the waiting area from the room where Sonia and I waited, and I could feel his tension in his tight shoulders and crossed arms. He was there as himself but he was also there as a proxy for my father. More than a shirt or a hat, that's how Walter Wright Thompson Sr. would witness the birth of his first grandchild, a little girl who would share his middle name and his initials. Another WWT. I wanted to tell Uncle Will I had noticed, not just his actions today but his actions through all these years, to let him know that I loved him, and that I so appreciated the burden he recognized and shouldered. That's a complicated thing to talk about. I worried I didn't have the words. Thankfully I wouldn't need words.

I reached into the bag and gripped the neck of the bottle and walked out to the waiting room. He saw me and leapt up and we embraced. Then I handed him the bottle. Tears filled his eyes and there wasn't a word that needed to be said. He took that bottle home and shares it with special people and on special occasions. I'm not sure what it means, but the last two gifts I've given Uncle Will were that bottle and a Thomas Merton book, because I like to talk about my evolving faith with him. There's synchronicity at work all around us. A few weeks later, a package arrived at my house from the Old Rip Van Winkle Distillery. I tore open the box and gasped. Julian had sent a hand-labeled bottle of whiskey to

Wallace, bearing her name and date of birth, safe in a plush red bag. It sits in my liquor cabinet, hopefully making the trip, waiting on a time when its presence is required to properly convey what a moment means, or what the people we are sharing that moment with mean, so we can revel in the great communal joy of being alive.

- Afterword -

by Julian Van Winkle III

THANK YOU SO MUCH for reading this little book about my life in the Kentucky whiskey business.

I definitely was not alone in making this brand a success.

After my dad passed away in 1981, I was in no position to run a business after working with him for only four years. So I would reach out to friends and others in the whiskey business when I needed help. I had two great ladies working for me as secretaries, Lois Devlin, who my dad hired after selling the distillery, and later Susan McCracken. They both helped me keep the business going.

When I purchased the old Hoffman distillery in Lawrenceburg in 1983, it consisted of a bottling house, a case goods warehouse, and one battered barrel-aging warehouse. Darlene Gillis came with the deal, thank God. She was a local and knew everyone in town. That helped when hiring people to work there. We even had the ex–Anderson County judge working on the bottling line. Getting people to show up for work was the hard part. During tobacco planting, picking, and stripping season, it was hard to get enough help for bottling. Darlene was friends with the local BATF (Bureau of Alcohol, Tobacco, and Firearms) inspector, which helped us immensely. She kept all the required government records along with precise bottling records of every bottle or decanter filled there. Since it was fifty miles from Louisville, I only went there when I needed to unload full barrels, process whiskey for bottling, or a thousand other tasks. She was there five days a week, except when she went to see her beloved Kentucky Wildcats basketball team in the SEC championship tournament. She would stay late waiting for truck drivers to pick up a few cases of whiskey going to my distributors. She would meet the county police at the bottling house or barrel warehouse, down a very scary Highway 44 in the middle of the night, when a raccoon, bat, or spider would set off the security alarm. I knew about it because she would call to let me know.

I could go on forever but, suffice it to say, this brand would not exist today without this lady and all the help she gave me over those nineteen years in Lawrenceburg.

My other savior in Lawrenceburg was Johnny Holzknecht. Johnny started working at Stitzel Weller for Pappy and my dad around 1950. By the time I began working there in the summers in the 60s, he had become plant manager. He knew every aspect of that place. After the distillery was sold in 1972 and Johnny retired, Dad hired him to make sure things were done correctly on the bottling line at Stitzel Weller when any Van Winkle bottles, including decanters, were filled there. I also desperately needed Johnny's help on the bottling line in Lawrenceburg after I bought the place.

He was invaluable in seeing how things should be done—things that I couldn't figure out for myself. I'd pick him up with his sandwich in a brown paper bag at 6:45 a.m. on my way to Lawrenceburg and drop him off at home later that afternoon. Thank God for Johnny Holzknecht! His daughter Carol Nord was hired by my dad in 1975 to hand-letter the names of customers in calligraphy on the front labels of our Old Rip personalized package. She must have inscribed her beautiful calligraphy on thousands of labels over the years. She just retired last year from that very important little job she did for me. Carol and her family were a big part of the success of our brand.

Gordon Hue's family owned a liquor store in Covington, Kentucky, just across the Ohio River from Cincinnati. He is the fellow that started the A. H. Hirsch Reserve Bourbon label, which I bottled for him in Lawrenceburg. Gordon used a couple of different bottles for his brand. One of them was the stock cognac bottle that I still use today. My first label using that bottle was my 12-year Special Reserve. The original label for that package was a knockoff of a private label owned by Darrell Corti, one of Gordon's liquor store customers in Sacramento. Darrell allowed me to use that label design for several years until I had it redesigned to the one I still use today. Gordon taught me not to be afraid to charge a higher price for a great bottle of whiskey. I was happy to get any price for my whiskey, but he taught me to take pride in what I was doing and get the money the whiskey in the bottle deserved. The two very famous and highly sought 14- and 16-year Stitzel-Weller–distilled

Van Winkle Family Reserve were Gordon's idea. It's people with these ideas who make me look good, and I really appreciate it.

Lance Bell ran his own ad agency in Saratoga, New York. He was frequently in Kentucky doing ad work for a couple of big-time horse farms near Lexington. Lance was stronger than new rope, sometimes not necessarily in a good way. My first contact with him was a phone call one day while Darlene and I were going over something in her dingy Lawrenceburg office. Lance's father-in-law had heard about our whiskey and wanted him to go by the "distillery" and pick up two cases of our 12-year, that day! I told Lance that it was a little more difficult than that due to the fact that our Kentucky distributor would have to ship it to a liquor store, and he would have to pick it up there. Nope, he was flying out that afternoon and needed it then. Long story short, Lance picked up the two cases and put them in the overhead on his flight back to New York. The good ole days before September 11.

Lance was wound tight and I was not. He was a go-getter and I was not. He was an idea man and I was only sometimes. For a few years I advertised in *Wired* magazine, *Whisky* magazine, and even the Churchill Downs racing program. He was a wheeler-dealer, getting me very low prices for magazine ad space. One day while sitting in the Lawrenceburg office, he pulled out a WSWA registration form from the trash where I had thrown it.

On that year, I didn't want to spend the money to set up at the yearly distributor/supplier trade show in Las Vegas. He would have none of it. I ended up going further in debt by spending a fortune renting furniture, Oriental rugs, chairs, etc., to create a mini "Pappy

Van Winkle study" as my display booth for this three-day show. The eye-catching setup worked in our favor. I picked up a couple of new distributors. We used this same very expensive but novel idea at the annual Kentucky Bourbon Festival in Bardstown, Kentucky. Pappy's study this time had bookshelves, wingback chairs, Oriental rugs, photos of the bottles, and Pappy's oil portrait, which I borrowed from Sally, hanging over a fireplace with artificial flames. This was all created for the black-tie, two-hour tasting that took place before the sit-down dinner dance. I was in the tasting tent with all the big boys: Beam, Buffalo Trace, Four Roses, and Maker's Mark. Our long line of people waiting to taste our whiskey, longer than anyone else's, was backed up all the way to the Maker's Mark booth across the room. I was loving it. Preston first got bourbon fever there. At least one of my girls and Sissy helped me pour and schmooze with the patrons. We used "Pappy's study" for several years after that, experiencing the same crowds of people eager to taste our whiskey. Thanks, Lance.

In 1986, I received a call from the office of Marci Tyson, now Marci Palatella. Her company, International Beverage, was an exporter of spirits to Japan. She wanted to sell our whiskey to her customers. She had her own bourbon label called Very Old St. Nick. I've never been clear on why that name was popular in Japan, but it was. Most of her Japanese distributors had requested a supply of very old bourbon, much older than what was available in the US. I bottled aged bulk whiskey that I had stored in my aging warehouse under her label and some of my own labels. It was a very nice piece of business. The profit margin for export was slim compared with the US market, but I was starving and it provided some cash flow. All along, she was saying that I should put Pappy's image on a label, and it would sell like crazy. I guess it was that idea she planted in the back of my head years earlier that led me to come up with the original 20-year Pappy label. The photo on that label was the one I found buried in a file cabinet in my basement in the early nineties. Eventually she asked me to look for some aged rye whiskey for her same customers. At the time, I don't believe I had ever tasted a Kentucky straight rye whiskey before, and neither had most of America. Fritz Maytag was making some young whiskeys from rye out in San Francisco under the Old Potrero label. That brand was gaining some traction in the US, but there were no older rye whiskeys on the market.

I found some 13-year-old Medley Distillery rye whiskey barrels for sale that were owned by United Distillers. The whiskey was incredible! One of my all-time favorite whiskeys. A year later, two New York area writers found out I was selling an aged Kentucky straight rye whiskey in Japan and told me that I needed to start selling it in the US market also. So thank you, Marci, for giving me the ideas.

Thank you, David Black. You are damn good at what you do!

Scott Moyers. When this book idea first came about, I was of course dubious. I have to thank Scott for his willingness and vision to be interested in this project from the get-go. This was a true leap of faith on his part from where I sit. Thank you, Scott!

People ask me all the time how and when did this whole VW whiskey mania begin. I'm not exactly sure, but I think it was sometime around when my friend Jimmy Hagood from Charleston introduced me to John Huey, who at the time was editor-in-chief of *Time*. He's into bourbon, so after trying ours he said he'd do a piece on me in *Fortune*. Sure, John! Well, he did not disappoint. That was in the February 2011 issue. David DiBenedetto and Rebecca Darwin published an article about me in *Garden & Gun* magazine in mid-2012. My recollection is that the timing of these two articles is the genesis of this whiskey craze for VW and me.

Having world-class chefs like Tony Bourdain, Sean Brock, John Currence, and Edward Lee talk up your booze sure didn't hurt. Word of mouth is the best advertising there is—pure and honest info from your friends on what to try and enjoy. I often jokingly ask people if they've ever told anyone about our whiskey. When they say yes, I say, "Well, there you go; you've created your own competition!" Our whiskey would show up in TV shows and movies without our knowledge. All these little pieces of the pyramid added up to the crazy popularity we are experiencing today.

Thanks to John T. Edge, director of the Southern Foodways Alliance. I am sure that is where the interest for a James Beard Award nomination came from. I also want to thank my friends Sam and Mary Celeste Beall, proprietors of Blackberry Farm. Over the years, they introduced me to many great chefs and wine vintners who perhaps may have given me a vote for that cherished James Beard Award in 2011.

Thanks to the powers that be at Buffalo Trace. In 2001, Preston and I, along with my attorney Vic Baltzell, were in negotiation for months with Chris McCrory and Steve Camisa who at the time were working at Buffalo Trace. I don't think our deal would have gotten done without their help. And of course Mark Brown's guidance and support then and for the last eighteen years has been so very much appreciated. Our main touchstone at the distillery for these past many years has been and still is Kris Comstock. His knowledge of the business and all his help in allocating our inventory each year is invaluable.

Wright Thompson is a wordsmith. When describing people or certain situations, he has a way of putting words together in a manner that is magical. You read one of his sentences and sit back and go, "Wow, how can anyone come up with that stuff?" It's been a thrill for me and Sissy to hang out with him over the last three years. He makes you feel as comfortable as an old pair of shoes. I had no idea how this whole book thing about me was going to go, but he nailed it. We have been on a parallel journey together regarding our relationships with our fathers. He has woven those personal feelings in his life into mine to present this story that is my life.

This is kind of like those award show moments when you could mention everyone who has helped you along the way but don't have the time—or pages—to do it. But I must mention just a few more briefly. I'm sure, just as those actors or musicians do, I'll miss a few. Sorry y'all.

Artist Ken McKiernan helped me design the Pappy label and a few other Van Winkle labels.

My dad's original Stitzel-Weller artist, Bob Wathen, designed our decanters and labels, including our original Old Rip label.

Thanks to my children for keeping me motivated when they were young, and helping me toe the line now that they are adults, and for giving us fabulous grandchildren.

Last but certainly not least is Sissy. Wright mentions her many times in this book because she was and is an integral part of any success that I have had. I have been bouncing ideas off her from the beginning. If I wanted an opinion about how good or bad a new whiskey was that I was considering selling, I had her try it. She has the best palate in the family and I trust it. It was tough for her to be alone from time to time raising four small kids. In the beginning, and even still today, she can hold her own at a whiskey show, cheerfully pouring a tiny amount of our whiskey for hundreds of attendees and chatting it up with all of them, making them feel like they are one of our family. Just recently, Preston was unavailable to attend Whisky-Fest San Francisco, so she filled in for the job of pouring. There were more pictures taken of me than ever because she was at my side. She's got that knack. Everyone is her best friend after meeting her, and that is a huge comfort and crutch for me. I'm shy and I think she would say that she is, too, but if you meet her, you would never know it.

I love you, Bud!

– Acknowledgments –

Wright Thompson

A long and strange process took this book from how it was first imagined (and sold) to the object in your hands. Five people are primarily responsible for shepherding it, and me, during this journey. I want to thank them first: Julian and Sissy Van Winkle; my editor, Scott Moyers; my agent, David Black (who first came up with this idea); and, of course, my wife, Sonia Thompson, who put up with this project happening while I already had a full-time job.

I want to thank my family for showing me how to move through the world: Uncles Rives, Rabbit, Will, Michael, and Frazier. All my cousins. My aunts Nan, Jennie, Becky, and Tempe. My brother, Willie. And, most of all, my dear sweet, smart, fierce, and kind mama. I love you, Mama.

I want to mention my father, who is gone and yet somehow alive on every page. Buying this book keeps him vital, and I cannot explain what a gift that is to me.

Thanks to everyone at Penguin, especially Mia, Sam, and Matt.

Thanks to Bill Simmons and Dan Fierman at the late and lamented Grantland, where I first wrote about Pappy.

Writing for a living means that while readers consume each work individually, they are all linked to me, small steps toward a distant destination, and therefore I want to make sure and acknowledge those who help me day in and day out, from my first job at the newspaper in New Orleans to my current position at ESPN.

Scott edited this book, and he made it immensely better, and he is in a long line of women and men who have looked after my words and, more important, looked after me: Colleen McMillar, Mike Fannin, Jay Lovinger, Paul Kix, and Eric Neel.

Eric is someone I talk to multiple times a day, at all sorts of inappropriate hours, so I also want to thank his family for their indulgence: his wife, Gwen, and the unstoppable Tess.

Working at ESPN means being involved in many different forms of storytelling, and being in airports and hotels with a band of fellow road warriors doing all that aforementioned storytelling. So a lot of people have seen me tapping away at this project while we traveled the country doing stories, and I appreciate their patience and guidance as I wrote and talked through the ideas and complications in this book. There's the Shelter Island crew: Tom Junod, Seth Wickersham, Kevin Van Valkenburg, and the ubiquitous Mr. Neel; our ongoing conversation about writing, literature, music, film, family, love, loss, joy, pain, and everything else good or bad we encounter in our day is centering and affirming for me. In a way, this book is just an extension of that conversation. There's Paul Kix, who did an invaluable read and edit. There is Tim Horgan at Bluefoot, who has become family to me. There's John T. Edge at *TrueSouth*, whose wisdom and friendship are reflected on nearly every page. The whole *TrueSouth* team: Dan, Hillary, Nicole, Angie, Shane, Steven, J. D., Thom, Vin, and Matt. Add Kaline and you've also got the Lil Wayne video team. I must thank the podcast ninjas: Courtney Harrell and Jess Hackel from Pineapple Street Media, which has become my Brooklyn home away from home. Their light and life have infused these pages, and I appreciate their friendship and hard work. And, of course, there are the folks back at the Mothership. I appreciate them all: Ali, Scott, James, Rachel, KJ, Jena, Rob, McQuade, Roz, Lee, Steph, Buckle, Connor, Dahl, Amanda, Drew, the whole Gameday crew, and many more.

Thank you to Wallace's godfathers: Clay Skipper and Rick Telander.

One last word about Seth Wickersham. For two decades, he has been my best friend and fellow traveler through this weird career we've both chosen. I can't begin to list the small and large ways he has influenced every word in this book, nor can I ever properly thank him for that help.

Finally, to Wallace: I spent a lot of nights away from you while reporting this book, and I want you to know, whenever you are old enough to read this, that every single day I was gone, I was thinking of you. In the end, this book is for you most of all. And let me save you some soul searching: you don't owe me anything. I love you completely and unconditionally.